Wasting Time With People?

ALICE LEAHY

Alice Leahy is director and co-founder of TRUST and a member of the Irish Human Rights Commission. Alice is a nurse and midwife as well as a writer, commentator, broadcaster and lecturer, with a special interest in promoting understanding about those who are excluded and combating social exclusion in all its forms. This is her third book, following *Not Just a Bed for the Night* (jointly written with Anne Dempsey) and *With Trust in Place*. She has received a number of awards over the years for her work with society's most disadvantaged people.

Wasting Time With People?

Compiled and edited by Alice Leahy

Gill & Macmillan

Gill & Macmillan Ltd
Hume Avenue, Park West, Dublin 12
with associated companies throughout the world
www.gillmacmillan.ie

© Contributions, the individual contributors, 2008
© Introduction and organisation, Trust 2008
978 07171 4480 8

Typography design by Make Communication
Print origination by Carole Lynch
Printed and bound by ColourBooks Ltd, Dublin

This book is typeset in Linotype Minion and Neue Helvetica.

The paper used in this book comes from the wood pulp of
managed forests. For every tree felled, at least one tree is
planted, thereby renewing natural resources.

5 4 3 2 1

This book is dedicated to James McCormick and Frank Purcell

The late Prof. James McCormick was an inspirational figure in Irish medicine, somebody who changed the lives of the many patients, students and colleagues who met him. In his long working life he was a family doctor, dean of the Faculty of Medicine and Professor of Community Health in Trinity College, Dublin, founding President of the Irish College of General Practitioners, chairman of the Eastern Health Board, author of many seminal papers and books on medicine, and long-time chairman of TRUST. Pomp and ceremony were not his thing: James preferred the currency of truth and companionship. This wisest of owls is now gone, but there remains a tree full of legacies that all who knew him cherish dearly.

The late Frank Purcell grew up in Co. Tipperary but spent most of his adult life in Dublin. He was passionate about Gaelic games, horse racing and motor sports. He played football for his local club, Moyle Rovers, and also for the Tipperary minor football team. He worked all his life in the motor trade in Dublin, winning the Bosch European Salesman of the Year Award in the late 1970s. He was a very successful businessman and was once described by a colleague as 'one of life's true gentlemen.' He knew of the work of TRUST and was a great friend of the organisation.

Contents

Acknowledgements

This book was possible because of the commitment and generosity of contributors, each of whom offered real dedication in meeting their deadlines. I want to thank each of them for writing something special; this hopefully will move more of us to make time for others. In acknowledging people I want to stress that this is why we sought to have this book published. It would not have been possible without the unstinting co-operation, enthusiasm and hard work of a great variety of people, in addition to the creativity and commitment of our contributors. All royalties from this publication will go to TRUST.

I would like to thank Fergal Tobin, our publisher, and his excellent team at Gill & Macmillan, who made the process such a pleasure; our trustees, who as usual were hugely supportive; and of course my colleagues in TRUST, without whom this project would not even have got to the starting gate.

Most of all, however, I would like to acknowledge the people we meet every day who inspired us to undertake this project. While it is true that we can offer them some help, it is also true that we get something in return, which can be of considerable value. This book in a real way reflects that: insights and understanding, not only about the human condition but even about the nature of society. Maybe it is true that the measure of a society is how it treats its most vulnerable citizens. However, to really understand a society and where it is going you also have to work with the most vulnerable, those who cannot, or will not, fit in in the mad rush for material success.

ALICE LEAHY
Director and co-founder
TRUST

Introduction

Dear Nurse Alice,

About three years ago through no fault of my own, I found myself in a homeless situation. I was addicted to neither drugs nor alcohol, yet I found myself wandering the streets of Dublin on a daily basis, sometimes not speaking to a soul for an entire week. I found out about TRUST *and was met by a nurse who allowed me to shower and have cups of tea, she then looked at my feet, they were very sore because of all the walking I was doing, she dressed them for several weeks and never complained once.*

TRUST *gave me back my dignity, albeit in a small way, I am now in my own accommodation for three years, and am a second year student at Trinity College. I am a 45 year old man who will always remember you and your staff.*

As a student I do not have much money to spare but I would like you to have the enclosed, it may buy some fruit or biscuits for your clients. I wish it was 500 times more. Keep up the good work.

Do we 'waste time with people' in TRUST?

Yes, and it is something we do every day, and in a very telling way it very much reflects the essence of our philosophy. And letters like the one above keep us going and help us to maintain our commitment to treating people as people and to giving them the time they are entitled to as human beings.

Of course it is untrue in the real or human sense that we 'waste' any time. In fact it is impossible for us to do that, as we believe time spent helping another person is of immeasurable and often indefinable value and not susceptible to easy measurement by conventional 'quantitative performance indicators'. We chose that question as the title of this book because it reflects the values and the language used by those who are committed to a management philosophy that seems to assert that you can achieve 'success' without devoting real time to helping people who are broken, vulnerable and outsiders in our society.

However, the importance of 'wasting' time with people was well understood by our late chairperson, Prof. James McCormick, one of the two people to whom this book is dedicated. One day he gave me an article from the *British Medical Journal* that impressed him on that theme, and a short quotation captures the essence of the piece. It was written by Simon Challand, a former medical adviser in Uganda, about the advice he had received from

> an African Bishop with a smile—'Waste time with people . . . You Europeans are always concerned about projects and budgets. The African does not worry about them—just waste time with people.' He gave me this advice in 1996 shortly before I came out to work in Uganda. Since then his words have kept coming back to me, and I reflect on their truth and wisdom and how difficult it has been for me, as someone with European values and attitudes, to apply them.

The writer was very honest about his difficulty in applying these words in practice, but I can easily identify with the African bishop, based on what I see happening daily. In the Ireland of today, while the country has definitely become more prosperous, one very unfortunate implication of this is that 'time is money,' and that seems to apply almost everywhere. For example, in providing someone with a public service—in health or in the area of homelessness—it can be difficult if not impossible to spend the necessary time helping them without coming up against a budget constraint. Indeed if we placed the emphasis on time for people rather than money we would live in a very different country, and that idea is quite challenging in a world governed by monetary budgets. In fact most people probably work very hard to maintain their standard of living, and such an idea, as they struggle to balance their own budgets, might appear at best well meaning and naïve and at worst unrealistic or even mad!

However, as we meet the everyday casualties of a society that could not make time for them we feel it is very important that we confront the implications of that situation; and we are privileged that such an amazing cross-section of people were prepared to spend some time in considering this issue with us, and we are extremely grateful to them.

Many realise the importance of spending time with people when it is too late—standing sometimes beside the coffin of a loved one, regretting the lost opportunities to be together that were squandered, not listening to what they had to say perhaps, wasted maybe in pursuit of some material or career goal. More than most, because we meet the victims every day, we know how devastating the failure to give time to others can be.

But we do have choices, even if our room for manoeuvre may appear slim. Indeed it would be wonderful if we could help initiate a national debate on this topic. There can be little doubt that if more of us were to spend more time with those we love or care about, and society placed a premium on time spent caring for others, especially if that quality of caring was extended to the services for those who cannot cope and find themselves homeless on the street, we would all be better off.

We try to do that. We try to live that philosophy of giving time to people. We try to provide a daily place of refuge for those who feel excluded by society. We do not ask them to fill in forms. We do not ask questions. If people choose to talk, we listen. We provide what health care we can in a holistic or, as we see it, in a personal and human way. A change of clothes; a shower—anything we can do to make a life on the outside a little more bearable, just by giving them time. The more we think about time in that context the more the word 'caring' seems to naturally emerge.

What we are really talking about is a philosophy of caring about people as people. This vision was very much responsible for the setting up of TRUST.

What is remarkable, and a little disturbing, about Ireland's new prosperity is how little has changed in people's attitudes towards the outsider since TRUST was founded in the mid-70s, when we first began visiting hostels, night shelters and people sleeping out in 'skippers' (derelict buildings, old tree trunks, abandoned cars—anywhere they found shelter) to provide what help we could. Today most professionals and managers manage the process from their desk and do not go out and meet people on the ground. The managers of the 'services' have become more and more remote from the people they serve, and time spent directly with people has become a scarce commodity.

The fundamental problem we seek to confront is that those managing the services appear to have lost touch. The more resources they employ the less impact they have, because those who should be consulted are not asked for their opinions, and views that are different are dismissed. Those, like us, who put the personal and human needs of people who are on the margins first are considered not to be progressive and are therefore dismissed.

This 'modern approach' to solving problems requires agencies to adopt quantitative or budget-based 'performance indicators' and to seek to make people who are homeless conform to 'benchmarks'—in short, to subject them to a level of 'management' that drove many of them out onto the street in the first place.

'Management' means forcing people to change, which many of them are simply not able to do. We are trying in this book to show that time given to people is what is important, not least in helping to ensure that those seeking help are not further excluded.

Some people working with those on the margins of society see the urgency of doing this but are not in a position to speak out, for fear of losing their job or seeing their agency having its funding cut—the latter an unfortunate consequence of the creeping privatisation of the state's services that has occurred in recent years. Mary Robinson, former President of Ireland, said in 2001: 'Each time you speak out with a critical voice you pay a price.' But should that have to be so in our public services? We have relentlessly advocated whistle-blower legislation that would offer real protection. Would recent scandals in nursing homes have been possible if such legislation existed, and a culture that encouraged people to speak out in defence of the most vulnerable?

To understand the importance of time for the people we meet it is important to understand the conditions many find themselves in. Every day we see people whose bodies are ravaged by disease and violence, and some with hearts and minds at breaking point. We meet men and women who have been abused mentally and physically, and some who may be working in prostitution. We see people who have been institutionalised in psychiatric hospitals and prisons for many years and then moved from one institution to another. We meet increasing numbers of people unable to express their sexuality freely and who then become almost suicidal and victims of intimidation and violence.

People who become homeless often suffer unexpressed guilt because they have left loved ones behind—women with children in care and frequently men barred from the family home; many with parents who have passed away and to whom they were unable to say goodbye; many with serious addiction problems, including gambling;

some heavily involved in drugs to blot out the pain of living; and many who have attempted suicide.

Recently we have seen large numbers of people coming from the EU accession states. Like the Irish who found that the streets of London or New York did not offer the opportunities they imagined, many end up on the streets when things go wrong. As the construction industry encounters problems, we will probably see the numbers increase further.

We also work hard to help people understand what it means to be an outsider in Irish society. In fact we are highly committed to our work as advocates for the outsider, and that is why we began our education and awareness activities, of which this book is a part. I would like to include some quotations from students after they saw our recent DVD, *Building Trust in the Community,* which was produced as part of our latest national initiative, aimed at community groups, to promote greater understanding about what it feels like to be left out or excluded in Irish society.

The strongest impression left with me after watching this DVD is the constant dehumanisation and loneliness that is experienced by people who find themselves living on the streets. I think this particularly struck a chord because every one of us is probably guilty at one instance or another of looking away when a homeless individual asks for help and perhaps not even acknowledging them . . .

As a student social worker, the video has given me the realisation that we need to examine whether we are driven by our desire to further our professional development or by our desire to offer our help to people.

What I and many others tend to forget is that the homeless are people, and, like all of us, they have a past and a future . . .

Have I moved away from this humanity in my training as a social worker? Do I talk more, think more of people as clients and less as human beings?

These people look educated, and why are they now on the streets?

As an overseas student in Ireland I've watched some documentary programmes about the common or average people's life in this society. However, today it is the first time I've been deeply touched.

I went to London this summer, and while we were out one night we met a homeless man from Dublin who was stuck there because he could not get home, and that's all he wanted to do. The video reminded me of him. He just wanted to come home.

It focused on angles that I never knew existed, i.e. the condition of homeless people's feet etc., rather than drink, begging etc.

If anything the DVD made me feel ashamed. I disregard any homeless person on the street, and while I might occasionally give them a euro or two I never fully think about them. I go on about my day to day and be done with them. We don't like to think about social problems on our own doorstep, so we associate with giving to charities concerned about Africa rather than charities in our own city.

This made me realise that I don't look homeless people in the eye as I pass them in the street, and that's wrong. For a short documentary it really changed my outlook . . .

These comments, like the letter I quoted at the beginning, we found extremely heartening and indeed inspiring, because they reminded us that we can make a difference for others, and we can give others the opportunity to make a difference by helping them to understand and appreciate what it means to be an outsider. However, our work would also not be possible but for the generosity of people from all walks of life who help us in many different ways to keep going, and we are very grateful for it, because through their support we are allowed to maintain our independence and to act as advocates for the outsider, as we do not receive state funds. At a time when a new form of privatisation of state services is under way, with the voluntary sector being contracted to undertake more and more services, our independence to speak out when it is important to do so is more important than ever.

Our work in the area of advocacy has also given us a much greater appreciation of the importance of seeking to ensure that all agencies working with vulnerable people adopt an approach based on human rights. One example of the degree to which people who are homeless are treated like second-class citizens was an assessment form created by the homeless agency, which was a staggering forty pages long, asking the most personal questions dealing with health, also seeking details about criminal records and related issues, and asking permission to share that information with other agencies! It was also suggested to us that the questionnaire had to be completed or the person would not receive a service. However, the Data Protection Commissioner thought this matter serious enough, when we brought it to his attention, to launch an investigation. It is difficult to convey the serious consequences such a questionnaire could have had if put to a vulnerable person suffering from a serious mental health condition by an inexperienced interviewer.

This book is dedicated to two special friends of TRUST, both of whom lived that very idea and who passed away recently and quite suddenly: our late and much-loved chairperson, Prof. James McCormick, whom I have already mentioned, and Frank Purcell from Co. Tipperary, a great friend and supporter of TRUST. Each of them in his own quite different way showed how a person could make a real difference for the outsider, and both of them knew the importance of time and what a difference it can mean to others.

A few years ago James wrote an essay entitled 'The Outsider', which is included in this book and gives a good insight into his understanding of that philosophy. Frank helped many people in a quiet and sensitive way, as the article about him here by Vincent (Jasper) Murphy shows. A good indication of his ability to inspire others is also revealed by the fact that his friends continue to organise the golf classic he helped found for us in his honour, the Frank Purcell Memorial Golf Classic for TRUST, in Fethard (my own home town).

This book is about sharing experiences and insights that hopefully will help us make a difference for others. We feel we owe a great debt to our contributors, because they have given us not only their time but a lot to think about. But giving time to others also implies listening, especially when a person needs such support, a fact that certainly made a difference to many of our contributors. Indeed the ability to listen—something the people who visit us value greatly—is underestimated. It can make a big difference when someone needs to get something off their chest, even a life-changing difference, especially if it prevents the making of an impetuous and spur-of-the-moment decision that could have serious consequences. This support we can all offer to each other.

Which brings me to a useful point to conclude on. We all gain, in all walks of life, if we give more time to each other. Advocating that we all waste more time with people is not only good for the people we meet every day in TRUST: it would be good for all of us. We can start a quiet revolution in Irish society that would alter the quality of life for almost everyone if we consciously decide to make a point of 'wasting' more time with each other, especially those we love and care about. Then, extend that support to those who did not get that love and support when they needed it and maybe today are struggling to make it on the street. This revolution definitely begins at home, and everyone can participate.

ALICE LEAHY

Time on my hands

Robbie

I am lost every day with so much time on my hands. After a serious accident I was in hospital for months and recovered slowly and now walk badly with crutches. Before that I was assaulted and had brain surgery; I was on a life support machine and was given a 5 per cent chance of survival—but I did. Some people thought I had died. The staff in the hospital were good to me.

Life is horrible at the minute: nothing to do but go to the clinic for methadone, go for a clean-up, often rushing to appointments and get there to find the person I was to meet doesn't turn up. The excuse is always the same: someone made a mistake, we forgot to tell you.

Sometimes people say it's my own fault. I agree and disagree. When growing up you can get involved in things because you want to be part of something. As you get older you think a lot, but you can't change the past. When you try to change you get laughed at and give up. If you have been in prison you are not allowed to forget it.

I am only in my forties but feel a lot older. I started taking drugs first at twelve or thirteen, smoking hash and then on to heavier drugs.

I went to two Christian Brothers' schools but rarely attended. I ended up in prison at age fourteen—Mountjoy. At that time you had to be sixteen to go to St Patrick's. In 1978 I was moved to Loughan House and escaped after a night out to see *Midnight Express*; it was on the paper.

I have spent most of my life in and out of prison. I have had relationships and children but they all broke up. One son is fostered, and I hope he gets a better chance than I did.

When in Mountjoy I kept my head down and went to school. I studied English and history and did my Leaving Certificate. I read and read in my cell and was on my own most of the time. Prison is a different world; from the time you go in you dream of getting out, and then you come out to what? Back with the same people and life-style. Drama in prison opened up a new life for me. I was in *Madigan's Lock* by Hugh Leonard and *Juno and the Paycock* and *Shadow of a Gunman* by Seán O'Casey. Claire and Lulu were great, and they all gave me something to look forward to. Mabel Troy was special, and Evelyn Lunney made me look like a star.

I have no plans for the future. If I get a decent place to stay maybe I could do something. Even though I have a lot of time, it takes all my time to get around and get through the day before I put my head down for the night—if I'm lucky enough to have a bed. I have today.

Robbie is a friend of TRUST.

Kebab and chips
Ronald

You could say I don't have a life. I will be sixty next year. I was always the black sheep of the family. My mother put me out of the house when I was eleven, and even then I slept in the back garden with the dog, in north Co. Dublin.

Looking back, I was a loner, and I have been drinking all my life. I married in Liverpool and lost my wife when she was in her twenties; she died of a brain haemorrhage. I had other relationships, and children, but have no contact with them.

During winter I visit my brother to get all the news. I stay a few hours and must keep windows and doors open; I cannot be locked up. I never went to school, I only went in to rob the buns left in the hall.

I ended up in prison a few times, here and in England, always drink-related petty crimes. The last time I was locked up was in 1969 in Mountjoy, and I won't be again.

I have no regrets—no good having regrets, is it? For the last eight years I have slept on a bench in a park in Dublin 4. I have lots of company there, visitors I suppose—you know them all yourself. I spend most days by the canal. I read a lot and get lots of books from a woman I meet there—you know I cannot spell, and at times cannot even write my name.

For about twenty years I worked as a plasterer in Jersey. I had to work there, there was no dole there.

You know, I would call myself an alcoholic. I cannot remember a morning getting up without a drink. At 5:30 a.m. this morning I was sitting by the canal with five cans—I always have a few for the morning. Some people can give up the drink, I can't, and I don't want to—I don't know what it does to me.

Once a week I go to TRUST for a shower and change; you could not exist without it, you would smell.

I don't need a mobile phone, I keep in touch with myself. When you go to get a service a lot of young people, some not Irish, don't understand you and why you sleep out. When they ask a lot of questions I just say, 'I don't know.' I am not prejudiced, and a lot of new people on the streets come from other countries. Some understand us, but we can't speak their language but will still understand each other and share a can.

I cannot handle responsibility. I refuse to go to hostels—too many rules, too many questions, and in some places you are scanned. You wouldn't get that in Mountjoy.

My friends are on the street, men and women. You can sit with them and have a yap; some have children they never see, and a lot have died.

I don't even know who is in Government; I think Bertie Ahern was for a bit. A man with a house and a job has no idea what it is like to be sleeping rough, or why someone would want to.

Some people are great. Last night a man in Donnybrook Abrakebabra gave me a €7 kebab and chips. I sat down in the park and shared them with the birds.

A few people I know got rooms, small with a bed, a chair and television. I couldn't go home to that; but they spend their time with their friends of before. I think we are all Park People, we love open spaces. You have the magpies at 6:30 a.m., the foxes, the ducks—but I think someone is stealing them, as there are less ducks in the park.

See, I still have the shakes, but I am clean now and will wander to the canal and watch the world go by. Some of my friends will be there, and the people I know going to work or walking their dogs will stop and have a chat. People are very good.

I suppose I am not like normal people, I just love out, that's my life.

I hope it doesn't rain. Someone robbed my umbrella.

Ronald is a friend of TRUST.

A welcome for strangers

Robert Ballagh

When I was a kid I think that the first serious reading that I indulged in, with the exception, of course, of the material prescribed by the Department of Education, was the work of John Steinbeck, and I'm pretty sure that it was his humane portrayal of the poor and the marginalised in the United States that awoke in me a concern for justice and human rights that has stayed with me to this day.

After Steinbeck I moved on to read Jack Kerouac, and I remember being struck by the freewheeling spirit displayed by the protagonists in his ground-breaking novel *On the Road*. In fact a friend and myself were so impressed by their 'devil-may-care' attitude that we decided on the spur of the moment to sally forth on the roads of Ireland and see where fate would take us!

We got the bus out to the Naas Road, stuck out our thumbs, and waited to find out what would happen. 'Where are you going, lads?' was the question posed by the first driver who stopped; he wasn't too impressed, however, by our reply, 'Wherever you're going' and immediately sped off without us. We decided on a different tactic with the next driver. Before he had a chance to even open his mouth we enquired about his destination, and on hearing 'Tipperary' we instantly replied, 'Oh, great, that's where we're going!' A few hours later we were deposited on the side of a road somewhere in Co. Tipperary.

We hadn't a clue where we were, so we decided to stroll along the road a bit to see if we could find our bearings. After a while we came upon a cottage with its front door open. I went up the path to see if anybody was at home. An old lady came to the door and asked if she could do anything for us. We admitted that we were lost and that we were just looking for directions. She insisted that we come inside, and I have to confess that any misgivings were instantly dispelled by the seductive smell of freshly baked bread emanating from the house. Once inside she immediately busied herself making a big pot of tea and cutting large slices off the enticing new loaf. She laid out the tea and bread, together with butter and jam, on the kitchen table and invited us to join her. Quick as a flash we tucked in to the spread and between gulpings and munchings discovered precisely where we were and where we should be headed. I vaguely remember that we continued our expedition to Cork, stayed one night and then hitched our way back to Dublin the next day. Some adventurers!

Almost fifty years have passed since we made that impromptu excursion, and, sadly, I'm fairly certain that the hospitality and the welcome for strangers that we experienced all those years ago would be hard to find in Ireland today.

Now I am not coming over all nostalgic for the so-called 'good old days,' because there were plenty of things about the old days that weren't so good at all. Nevertheless I just wish that the welcome rise in living standards that many of us are experiencing should not have to be at the expense of more benevolent human behaviour.

In my opinion, Ireland would be a far better place for all of us if we chose to be a little less self-centred and greedy and a bit more caring of others and certainly more willing to offer a sincere welcome to strangers.

Robert Ballagh was born in Dublin in 1943 and graduated from the Dublin Institute of Technology. He is both a painter and a designer. His painting style was strongly influenced by pop art, and his paintings are often playful and didactic. In 1991 he was the co-ordinator of the seventy-fifth anniversary commemoration of the 1916 Rising. Interviewed in the *Irish Times* on the ninetieth anniversary, he related that this had caused him to be harassed by the Special Branch of the Garda Síochána. Ballagh represented Ireland at the Paris Biennale of 1969. Among the theatre sets he has designed are sets for *Riverdance*, Samuel Beckett's *Endgame* (1991), and Oscar Wilde's *Salomé* (1998). He designed more than seventy postage stamps and also the last series of Irish banknotes, 'Series C', before the introduction of the euro. He is a member of Aosdána.

Unholy trinity

Siobhán Barry

As I finally sit down to write this piece, within hours of the deadline, I think back with some regret on the weeks that I had this topic on my back burner, being idly mulled over when perhaps I should have been more focused on the task of committing my thoughts to paper. Should I have scribbled down the first ideas that came to mind on the subject and at this late stage hope that I haven't mistaken my inactive contemplation with procrastination, or now with anxious over-analysis, so that all spontaneity of thought is lost?

I consider, with some anticipatory embarrassment, that my thoughts on the theme may be considered very pedestrian by the editor and that her blue pen may not be able to elevate my jottings to the novel or unique that she is expecting to ignite a debate. But then I comfort myself with the fact that a broad range of people have been invited to contribute to this book, and perhaps my little offering might be concealed among their great insights. Anyway, don't debates usually induce a degree of vacillation?

Over the past fifty years, services for people with psychiatric illness have gradually moved from being custodial and institutional in nature to what are now termed 'community-based' mental health services. In some ways this was a positive change, compared with the drab and austere Victorian mental asylum of the past that was the receptacle of those with psychiatric illness, for which there were few effective interventions, and also those with a wide range of other life situations, from social deviance and 'illegitimate' motherhood to those with epilepsy and mental handicap. However, notwithstanding the patchwork of people placed in those mental hospitals, residents were at least able to take as a given the asylum or refuge aspect of such care, meagre and basic as it was. Today there are few safe havens for people who are troubled and dispirited.

Nowadays we are frequently told that one in four of us will encounter mental health difficulties over the course of our lifetime, and also that more than 90 per cent of those mental health difficulties are treated in general practice. At one level these figures serve to demystify the occurrence of mental health difficulties within the general population. Unfortunately, however, such bland statistics don't help to inform us of the nature and course of chronic and enduring psychiatric illness, which forms a small sub-set of those who are covered by the umbrella term of mental health difficulties, or how the quality of life of people thus afflicted could be improved.

In January 2006 a new national mental health policy, *A Vision for Change*, was launched following a long and widespread consultation process. This set out a blueprint for the development of the mental health service for the subsequent seven to ten years. Over several chapters the vision underlying this policy was set out; the plan for the development of the service was explained in further sections; and finally the process of implementing this policy was outlined. Psychiatric services for children, for those with learning disabilities, for adults with serious mental illness, for older people and special subgroups, such as the homeless, for those with substance abuse problems and those with forensic histories, were meticulously described; and for a period there was a frisson of excitement at this new dawn of enlightenment in the organisation and provision of service that was to be translated into action.

An independent monitoring group, however, has been quite scathing in its report in May 2007 about the slow progress made in implementing this policy, and the 'unholy trinity' of the health services has reared its head: services being overpromised, being underfunded, and the blame shifted when failures become apparent.

Psychiatric services are under serious pressure. The demands vary from urban to rural areas, and this sense of being under stress is picked up by patients. In urban areas, in-patient beds tend to be in short supply, and retaining staff members in the Dublin area is difficult, because of the high cost of living and a consequent adverse knock-on effect on continuity of care. In some rural areas large institutions flourish, but services in the community tend to be poorly developed, with little by way of follow-up care once people are discharged from hospital. There is a huge mission leach in psychiatric services, and often vague mental health difficulties are cited to evade the law or to put pressure on the local authority to expedite accommodation—a cynical exploitation by the more able of service providers but at a cost to the more seriously disabled, whose needs are overlooked by such distractions.

If we want to provide humane and responsive care for individuals with psychiatric illness we will need to ensure that our national mental health policy does not become solely a well-written reference book. Enabling resources will need to be allocated. We need to invest in our futures and must not lose heart. This can be done.

Siobhán Barry is clinical director of the Cluain Mhuire mental health service in Blackrock, Co. Dublin, and public relations officer of the Irish Psychiatric Association.

Beth and Kitty

Maeve Binchy

B eth tried to be friendly when John and Kitty, the new people, came to live next door at number 29. She made them a lamb stew as a supper for their first night there.

They were polite and thanked her for her kind gesture, but they sent out a very strong message. They were very busy people, no time to waste by stopping to eat a dinner, and by implication no time to waste talking to neighbours.

Beth shrugged to herself. They had each other, John and Kitty, they had their high-flying jobs; why should they waste their most important currency—time?

And as the weeks went by she caught very fleeting glimpses of them. They always waved but never paused.

Kitty once said it must be *lovely* to be like Beth and not go out to work every day. But Beth knew that Kitty would curl up and die if she had to waste her time being in the house instead of going out and changing the world.

The man in the corner shop died, and Beth thought John and Kitty would like to know the time of the funeral, so she left a note in their house.

Some days later John paused for three seconds to say he was so sorry but they didn't want to waste time going to a funeral where they would know nobody and where their presence wouldn't do anything to help. But *so* good of Beth to let them know.

The months went by. Beth watched the comings and goings at number 29 from her kitchen window.

They never sat in their lovely garden. Once a month a firm of contract gardeners came to give it a little tidy up, as Kitty said. So much better to let professionals do it than wasting time with people, listening to their aches and pains and interminable stories of their travels on package tours.

They didn't have parties or dinners or friends around to sit in their big conservatory. They didn't join in the sponsored walk in aid of Famine, they didn't buy tickets for the coach tour of Magnificent Gardens, they didn't come to the switching on of the Christmas lights, and Beth advised against asking them to help with Meals on Wheels, teaching English to immigrants, or the pensioners' party.

She hated hearing them explain that they hadn't the time to waste on such works, worthwhile as they undoubtedly were. It annoyed her and made her dislike them.

Once she had overheard them talking about her. They called her that harmless poor bun-faced woman next door who had nothing to do with her time. Beth knew that listeners never hear any good about themselves. She examined her face in the mirror, decided it wasn't remotely like a bun, and decided to forget the remark. Beth was a happy person; she preferred liking people to disliking them.

And anyway, despite what they said, she actually had plenty to do. Beth got a nice hot breakfast for three elderly neighbours, a bacon sandwich and a mug of tea. She had keys to all their houses. Then she went to help in the day centre for two hours, then she did meals on wheels, in the afternoon she had slow learners for reading classes and four Polish girls for English lessons, at teatime she and her friend Maggie addressed envelopes for a charity (it was much easier these days because they had sticky labels), and every evening there was one thing or the other. At weekends she worked in a charity shop and she helped some of the older people in their gardens.

The day wasn't long enough; it was full of people; but she never felt that one moment of it was wasted.

The drunk who careered down the road and ploughed into numbers 28 and 29 hit Beth and Kitty very hard. The ambulance was called, and they ended up in the same ward. Kitty had a broken leg and Beth had a broken arm.

From Kitty's bed she watched as a stream of visitors came in to visit Beth—the woman with a face like a currant bun. Some were taking home her nighties to wash, others were bringing magazines, flowers from her garden, and mainly assurances that all the many aspects of her life were going along as she would have wished.

Someone else was making the bacon sandwiches and wondered should the rashers be well cooked or juicy. A man was teaching the Polish girls English, but he said he wasn't sure if they were satisfied because he spent too long on the off-side rule in soccer while they wanted more about clothes.

Kitty got a bouquet from the office, and John came in every night. There was talk about moving her to a private room, but she said she would prefer to stay where she was. Not only had the drunk broken her leg but the accident had also opened her eyes.

One night when John was visiting she asked him to water Beth's garden for her.

'I thought you said that you didn't want to waste time with people?' he hissed at her.

Kitty closed her eyes. Her face seemed to say that her husband had a lot to learn.

Maeve Binchy is an author, born in Dublin, who has written many best-selling books. They have been translated into more than forty languages, and several have been adapted as films, including *Circle of Friends, Tara Road,* and *How About You?*

Sudoku

William Binchy

We should be a bit slow to criticise others for wasting time. Just as one person's weed is another's flower, so our choices about how to spend our time vary hugely. I may think your golf handicap of five is evidence of too many summers frittered away in useless, if healthy, exercise; you may consider my expertise in *sudoku* conclusive evidence of a sad, solitary and unfulfilled life. The truth is that, outside family and work, human beings find fulfilment in a wide range of activities. There is simply no point in ranking them on some scale of worth.

Does this mean that it's impossible to waste time? Surely not. We all have thrown away time in failing to advance some cherished goal. We can become transfixed into stasis by an emotional barrier that prevents us doing well when we want to do excellently. Even as we recognise the vanity involved, the desire for achieving the best prevents us from settling for the adequate.

I come from a generation in which the language about wasting time was harsh and judgemental: 'sloth' and 'idleness' were words in common currency. Today they are used only ironically. Yet today the pace is far more frenetic than it was when I was growing up. The teachers may have railed against indolence and other Victorian vices, but my recollection is of time happily passed doing nothing very much. Homework was started on the train going home from Lansdowne Road; on a taxing day enough was completed by Blackrock station to reduce to nil the risk of exposure to the 'biffer'. Looking back, part of me wishes I had tried harder and had been more open to cultural and intellectual engagement. Another part of me defends those lazy years. They involved a secure environment for experiencing a range of human interchanges and working out slowly the true meaning of human qualities, good and bad, in myself and others.

In my adult working life I have discovered an odd fact about time. If you ration it when meeting those facing some problem that needs to be addressed, your discussion tends to be edgy and unfinished. If you make the decision to give whatever time is necessary to deal with the difficulty, something very positive happens. The other person picks up on that attitude. It tends to give assurance and encouragement. The problem can be addressed openly. Within a relatively short time, some way forward can be found. The result is far better and generally not more time-consuming than the scheduled twenty-minute interview slot.

The harder challenge is to reconcile the demands of work with the need to give time to family and friends. I remember reading on a fridge magnet in the American Mid-West thirty years ago the somewhat twee, but surely sensible, advice that 'if you've no time for your family and friends, you're busier than God wants you to be.' Getting that balance is not easy, and the advocate in our head for doing more work can be truly eloquent. If only we could have the wisdom to give work its proper place in our life our relationships would be much more fulfilling and our humanity that much more enriched.

William Binchy is regius professor of laws in Trinity College, Dublin, and a member of the Irish Human Rights Commission. He is a former special legal adviser on family law reform to the Department of Justice and has served as a research counsellor to the Law Reform Commission on the law relating to the status of children. He has contributed to public discussion of human rights issues, including those relating to Travellers, asylum-seekers, divorce, and abortion. He is the organiser of a programme on constitutionalism for the Tanzanian judiciary and since 1995 organiser of an annual workshop on constitutionalism for the chief justices and senior judiciary of African states.

Time is flying

Father Harry Bohan

lice Leahy's letter of invitation to contribute to this book poses important questions about how we use our time. There is no doubt that words and phrases that describe us and the way we live our lives these days are 'busyness,' 'time is flying,' and so on.

There are two systems that guide and shape our lives; one is economic and the other moral. The economic system belongs to the market. Its values are commercial values, and its language tends to dominate current affairs programmes and indeed everyday conversation. It tends to be about 'the price of everything and the value of nothing.' The price of land, houses and mortgages—these alone not only occupy a big part of public debate but also take care of at least a third of a couple's disposable income and the amount of time they spend at work to earn that income.

The moral system, on the other hand, belongs to the world of relationships: family, community, friends, children, elderly; relationships with inner self, creation, Creator.

When the economic system supersedes the moral system, when a society becomes totally preoccupied with economic and material worlds, people get very busy, very conditioned to define themselves by what they own. The world of relationships is sacrificed on the altar of growth—economic growth.

The fact is that the second half of the last century was about the material. The twenty-first century will have to tackle the world of relationships. Events are now bringing home to us the fact that our 'time-poor' world is having serious consequences for a lot of people.

Children are screaming for their parents' time; teenagers want to be heard, they want to tell their stories; old people, alone and lonely, do not need our busyness, only our time; husbands and wives cannot buy one another's respect.

It is east to go on and on. Our work in the Céifin Centre for Values-Led Change over the last ten years has indicated some of the issues emerging. One of these is that we are now confronted with problems we have no history, no experience, of dealing with. They are new to us; and the 'time-poor' problem is one of them.

The solutions must begin with identifying the issues. The debate is vital, because without the debate we lose the language of relationships. But we need to move to action, and we need organisations and institutions to engage seriously in reforming themselves in order to respond to the cries of people.

There is no doubt, as a consumer society, we are reaching saturation. Many people cannot take any more.

I believe a time-poor society is posing a question for education. Is it about preparing people for careers or for life, or can it be both? Can parents continue to hand over their children from a very early age to somebody else to at least part-rear them?

Does organised religion need to be seriously reorganised if it is to connect to the reality of people's lives? Do corporations need to take their responsibility to family and community seriously? And does the government need to realise that participative public life is as important as representative politics? Finally, do we urgently need to address the fact that massive amounts of money are being transferred from huge numbers of young people to a few very wealthy developers, resulting in massive pressure on family life?

If we are to put relationships and the moral system back into the heart of society we cannot continue to commercialise these relationships. We cannot sacrifice kinship, neighbourliness, shared cultural interests, religious affiliation, civic involvement on the altar of commercial transactions.

Economic progress has given us a freedom we never dreamed of. We are now free to choose. A freedom with meaning is the challenge that lies ahead.

Father Harry Bohan is a sociologist and parish priest of Six-Mile-Bridge, Co. Clare, director of pastoral planning for the diocese of Killaloe, and chairman of Céifin Centre for Values-Led Change. Recognised as a leading social commentator, he has written and broadcast extensively and was appointed by the Taoiseach to the Task Force on Active Citizenship. He is well known for his interest in sport, particularly Clare hurling.

Mount Saint Joseph

Conor Brady

Mount Saint Joseph Abbey lies about two miles off the main Dublin–Limerick road, near Roscrea. As you drive towards Nenagh you might catch a glimpse of the Abbey spire away to the north.

The Cistercian monks of the Strict Observance, or 'Trappists', have been here since 1878. Uniquely, among more than two hundred Trappist abbeys around the world, this one has a boarding school alongside it. I was educated there. For me it has always been a special place, and the Cistercian ethos has always been an important influence in my life.

Looking back over more than thirty years as a journalist and an editor, and looking forward to a world suffused with media, I appreciate Mount Saint Joseph more than ever.

The Cistercian way of life is based on the Rule of Saint Benedict. The Rule requires monks to divide their lives between work, study and prayer. It also enjoins them to offer hospitality and shelter. Mount Saint Joseph, therefore, like every other Cistercian foundation, maintains a guest house, where all are welcome.

Food is simple but good. The rooms, for those who stay, are comfortable and well equipped. The visitor may offer a donation, but nobody will be sent away because they have no money. Not too many questions will be asked.

But for those who want it there will be company and conversation. Monks are good listeners. There can be a wonderful silence too. A great deal of healing and of pouring out of troubles takes place in the Abbey guest house, in the walks across the Abbey farm or, indeed, in the confessionals at the end of the great Gothic nave of the Abbey church itself.

Mount Saint Joseph and other houses like it remain as islands of human communication in a world where people find it increasingly difficult to spend time in silence or to get other people to listen, or indeed to hear themselves think.

It is a place in which people experience the reality of interpersonal connectivity—as distinct from the many forms of 'virtual' contact that characterise contemporary western society.

Half a century ago the great Canadian guru of media theory, Marshall McLuhan, envisaged technologies and a world in which human interconnectivity would be total. He wrote of the 'global village', in which every person's experiences would be connected to everyone else's by the wonderful new technologies of broadcasting.

The technologies of McLuhan's 'global village' have become reality. Indeed what he foresaw has become *a fortiori* the reality of 21st-century Western life.

What he did not anticipate was the paradox that the more we were to become connected through these new technologies the more isolated, in human terms, we would be. In a world filled with iPods, mobile phones, blogs, mediated messages, broadcasts and on-line networks, flesh-and-blood interconnectivity between people becomes ever more a rarity.

Represented or mediated reality increasingly displaces experienced reality. People take decisions and form values, increasingly, not on what they experience themselves but on the basis of information that is 'mediated' to them by web-site designers, programme directors and editors.

Represented or mediated reality is faster, more efficient, more versatile and sometimes more persuasive than experienced reality. It takes time—it wastes time—to make connections with people in the real world. So connections are made in the mediated or virtual world.

Nowhere is the negative impact of this more clearly apparent than in the area of news journalism, in which I worked as reporter, broadcasting presenter and editor since leaving university in the late 1960s.

Somewhere—I fix it in the mid-1990s—an organic change began in many of the larger news media organisations in the United States. The television news companies, the newspapers and the radio stations started to come under the control of large conglomerates with interests in many businesses: hotels, entertainment, airlines, food products and so on.

And when the accountants at the corporate headquarters began to analyse the profit-and-loss figures they realised that the news industry was not as profitable as selling bed-nights or popcorn. The return on capital and the 'productivity' of news organisations were low and out of line with 'normal' earnings in other sectors.

News—accurate, balanced, reliable news—is expensive. Skilled journalists and editors are costly. They need to work on the ground, witnessing the events and talking to the people who make the news. Checking facts is costly. Weeks and perhaps months spent in investigative journalism are gall and vinegar to people obsessed with hammering down costs and boosting profits.

So the accountants and the managers began to hack down the costs. Overseas news bureaus were closed. Travel budgets were cut. News time was to be filled by using the telephone, syndicated services, and the internet. Production and editing were to be 'outsourced' to less-skilled workers, who cost less than traditional editors or directors.

These changes started in the United States; within a few short years they were being replicated in Europe and elsewhere. Virtually all European newspapers and broadcasters have cut back on their overseas commitments; they have reduced the numbers of their news staff; they have replaced news with 'infotainment' in very many instances; they have pinned journalists to screens in newsrooms rather than allowing them to get out to where the news is actually happening.

The new technologies of internet communication facilitate this. Broadcasting schedules can be delivered and newspaper pages can be filled without wasting a lot of time in conversation with people, without seeing what is happening on the ground and without putting pressure on journalists to call people who may be in the news in order to hear their side of the story.

It goes without saying that this phenomenon is more apparent in some media than others. The tabloid press and the 'middle-market' newspapers reflect it very clearly. More serious news media try to minimise its impact; but it is discernible even in the most reflective and purposeful newspapers and in the most 'public-service' oriented broadcasting organisations.

It is a sad pass for journalism, for journalists and for the general public who rely upon the news media for accurate information on important issues.

I do not blame the journalists, for the most part, although there are many whom it suits very well. Journalists work within the corporate policies that are shaped by those who control the news organisations. They work to ever-tighter deadlines and budgets, in the name of 'productivity'.

Meanwhile, back at Mount Saint Joseph, the Cistercians don't know much about productivity. Yet they know a lot about finding truth and about the necessity for dialogue among human beings. But between that sort of world and the world of modern news media there is simply no shared agenda. And I can see no possibility of any. The news media will continue to move to what can only be called a 'post-human-contact' phase. There will be less and less of 'wasting time with people.'

Conor Brady was editor of the *Irish Times* from 1986 to 2002. He is now a member of the Garda Síochána Ombudsman Commission.

Stroll with my dog

Jenny Bulbulia

The deadline for the contribution to this book is fast approaching—or even passed? With a niggling feeling of negligence and a certain degree of guilt I reopen the e-mail, sent long ago, inviting me to participate in this extraordinary project. To my surprise, the title of the book is *Wasting Time with People?* I had thought the title was *Making Time with People.* My mis-remembering is perhaps the point—and the problem.

I have a career, as a barrister, that affords me the privilege of encountering many different types of people. I have the further privilege of being a member of the Board of the Irish Red Cross Society, which allows me to engage with concerns of a humanitarian nature both at the national and the international level. However, the common thread that these have is that I have chosen for them to occupy my time. My choice; my terms. For the former I receive financial gain, and for the latter, satisfaction and personal growth. My choice; my terms.

However, there is a little bit of my day, every day, when commercial imperatives and humanitarian ideals are of little moment. It is my walk with my dog, in a park beside where I live. I moved here five years ago—an outsider. Having an Irish setter, I needed to exercise her fully and regularly if I was to keep her in the city; and she is my best friend. So we hit the park, day after day after day—encountering the ladies who lunch, the men who have the dinner in the middle of the day and the lads who drink their cans in the park from early morning.

We walked, and we walked. And then we made friends. The friendships are different with all the individuals. But what the friendships have in common is that they are uncomplicated. And they are friendships on equal terms. All these groups of people, collectively and individually, have chosen to welcome me to their park, their community, and their life.

I miss one of the men who I would meet in the early morning—I, having spent my night in bed, he, having spent his night in the park. 'Put your face to the sun, Jenny, and your shadow will always fall behind you,' he would say with sincerity and cheer and proceed to quote a poem that would uplift the spirit. A great way to start off the day; thank you for that!

And recently I met one of my favourite men from the park in a nearby off-licence on a Friday night. We were both purchasing the 'essentials'. He commented on the fact that I was buying wine. 'Jenny,' he said, 'you like wine. Have you ever tried Blossom Hill? I had a lovely bottle of it the other night with some roast chicken—you know the cooked ones they sell in Tesco.' Then he went on: 'What do you think of the concert tonight?—Rod Stewart. I've been at some of the best, but this guy is good. I'm surprised you're not down in the park yourself, listening to him.' I went straight to the local supermarket and bought a chicken, opened a bottle of wine, and, with a friend, sat out in my yard and did listen to Rod Stewart in concert.

On the weekends I travel further from the park, down to the canal, and meet the same lads who, with cheer and friendship, say, 'Morning. You've travelled,' and I say, 'Morning. So have you.' And then we'll chat about whatever we chat about: football, the weather, politics, or sometimes nothing at all.

These are my people; this is my community. We all have a choice in that regard. But choosing this is a mutual process, and it has to be a meeting of equals; then everyone benefits. And when we let people in and share a little of ourselves we can sometimes find that the 'ladies who lunch' don't often actually lunch—work and other commitments filling their days—but they become friends and people to share the ups and downs of the week with; and the 'men who have the dinner in the middle of the day' are wonderful neighbours who would do you a turn at a moment's notice (and sometimes have good tips for the horses); and the 'lads who drink their cans in the park from early morning' are real stars, whose good humour is infectious and their slagging, at times, unmerciful!

What we all have in common is a sense of community. The challenge is to remember this fact after we have left the park and enter the day-to-day stress of life. So let's *make time* with people, wherever we are and however busy we are, and simply see how we get on. 'Waste' is such a hollow word.

Jenny Bulbulia is a barrister at law and honorary secretary of the Irish Red Cross Society.

Getting involved

Maureen Cairnduff

Where I was born and grew up, in west Limerick, time was elastic. Neighbours were as important as crops. It was a small, close society—some might say too close: a sneeze could be heard in the next parish.

Newspapers were not needed for births, marriages or deaths, nor for weather forecasts and certainly not for gossip columns. People talked. They popped into each other's houses. A kettle was always on the boil, work was laid aside and time was made. Without modern appliances, time was precious, but listening to a friend was never considered a waste. Despite e-mail, mobile phones and text messages, communications seem to have broken down. Do people actually listen?

A country upbringing shapes our future. If I see someone looking a bit lost in the street or alone in a crowd, I try to help. I have to say that half the time help is neither needed nor wanted—a bit embarrassing. My late husband, who was not fired by my endless curiosity about people, constantly admonished me, 'Don't get involved!' A number of years ago I unwittingly became involved in a notorious kidnapping across the road from our house. It was in the middle of the night, so I invited the gardaí in, as you would. When my husband, on a business trip to Cork, turned on the morning news he heard me being interviewed. That evening, while listening to a Russian orchestra in the concert hall, he turned to me and said, 'Maureen, if any of them want to defect this evening, don't get involved!'

Recently I read the diary he kept of his cancer treatment. The recurring theme is his frustration at the lack of time he was given to communicate with his consultant.

Reticence can be commendable, but, looking back over my decades of 'getting involved' on planes and buses and in supermarket queues, I only regret the times I refrained from a friendly word or a helping hand. I am not totally unselfish in my desire to make strangers feel at home: at the back of my mind is the hope that someone, somewhere, will one day do the same for one of my family.

Maureen Cairnduff is a writer and journalist, born in Rathkeale, Co. Limerick. She was educated at Loreto Abbey, Rathfarnham, Co. Dublin, at the Priory, Haywards Heath, Sussex, and at the University of Madrid. She is a former columnist with the *Sunday Press,* editor and publisher of *Who's Who in Ireland* (1984, 1989, and 1999) and the author of *Exquisite Behaviour* (1995). A frequent contributor to newspapers, magazines, radio and television, she is also a member of the National Tourism Authority.

What did you do at the weekend?

Robert P. Chester

It was coming near the end of the month, and as it was my turn to spring for lunch I sent a text message to Frank. 'Lunch Tuesday 12.45 usual place, Rob.'

'Yep,' came the lengthy reply.

The place was a small, fashionable bistro serving overpriced food to rushed business types, many seeming to take about twenty minutes to drop the coat, order, swallow, pay and leave. We settled into a corner on a large, low sofa, very comfortable but going to be a challenge to eat from when the grub eventually arrived. Outside, the traffic was stationary.

'So, how's things?' I asked.

'Great.'

'Busy?'

'You know yourself . . . clients; I actually had to turn the bloody mobile off to get some work done.'

'It never ends, I suppose,' I commiserated.

'Yeah.'

'What did you do at the weekend?' I enquired.

'Oh, the usual. Met Pat and Jimmy for a couple of pints on Friday—went on a bit too late, though. Saturday was the usual taxi service for the sprogs, and her mother arrived looking for dinner; ended up cooking for the whole lot. Oh, I tried to get Pat to go golfing on Sunday but the football was rescheduled, so I picked up the presents for the party next weekend. Had to get out the laptop after I got the kids to bed to do that presentation for Monday morning . . . Are you going to the party?'

'Might make it, all right,' I said.

'What were you at for the weekend?' Frank asked.

'Well, I took the boat out on Saturday, went up to the lake, dropped the anchor . . . and came home on Sunday.'

'Great!' he said. 'Whatcha do?'

'I told yeh: boat up the lake, anchored for the day, came back on Sunday.'

'Did a spot of fishing?' he enquired.

'Nope.'

'Did you meet anyone up there?'

'Eh . . . no.'

'I bet you went into Carrick for dinner.'

'No . . . Ate on the boat.'

'Did you finish the book I gave yeh?' He was getting frustrated.

'No-o-o-o.'

'That was some weekend!' he laughed. 'You did nothing!'

'Well, actually, I suppose you're right . . . and wrong.'

I was going to explain to him that I had fulfilled a wish I had had for quite some time, an experiment in ways. I wanted to fill the time last weekend with me . . . just me and time. But the food arrived, interrupting the flow, and we moved on to other topics: our kids, house prices, rugby, and his dad's stay in hospital.

After, I didn't want to revisit last weekend, a weekend that flew in for me but it would be hard to show how.

I had spent almost thirty-six hours alone, and in considerable silence, except for the phone call to check that I hadn't fallen overboard. I left the radio off and cooked small meals of pasta and rice. I sat on deck and looked out over the lake for long periods, the occasional passing car on the lake road or lone tractor in a distant field the only disturbance.

When it had got colder in the evening I pulled a duvet around me and watched the sun go down, company consisting of a grey egret that had settled on a nearby marker buoy. Surprisingly tired after such inactivity, I crawled into the bunk, clothes still on, and drifted off with the slap, slap, slap of water on the side of the boat.

In the morning a mist cut visibility to a few feet in all directions, so I watched it slowly clear with a cup of warm milk, again wrapped up out on deck.

Later, heading back to the marina, I kept the little boat at its lowest speed, not wanting the time to end. After tying up at the pontoon I left, glancing back towards the lake, apprehensive of the return home.

I lost confidence in telling Frank this, feeling he might see it as selfish or perhaps even a bit odd.

Suddenly he said, 'Jesus, I'd love some time to myself.'

'Really? What would you do?'

'Don't know,' he replied, looking outside at the traffic, still stationary.

'Could you do nothing?' I asked.

'Absolutely *nothing?*' He sounded surprised.

'Yep!' I pressed.

'Don't know, never tried it. Even when I have the time I always seem to end up doing something,' he said.

'It's actually hard work doing nothing,' I said, my resolve to explain last weekend weakening.

'Sounds a bit lazy to me. If I had some time to myself I think I'd do something!'

'Oh,' I blurted, my resolve returning.

'Anyway,' his voice lowering, 'it'll never happen.'

The bill arrived, which I dutifully paid.

We parted at the door and agreed to meet for a drink before next week's party. As I moved towards my car, parked around the corner, Frank appeared beside me. 'Listen,' he said, slightly out of breath from catching up. 'We'll arrange to go up to the lake later in the summer. Might try some of this "quality time on your own" business.'

'Great,' I said.

'Okay, see yeh next weekend,' and off he rushed, not seeing the obvious.

I turned and walked across the road through the stationary traffic.

Robert P. Chester has worked for Dublin City Council for twenty-five years as an estate manager, senior community development officer and co-ordinator of the RAPID programme and is now manager of the Passport for Leisure scheme. He is also a well-known musician and conductor and at present is musical director of Knocklyon Concert Band Society, which he founded in 1998. He has won numerous national and international awards, and his All-Star Jazz Band was voted best dance band in both 2006 and 2007 at the Irish National Band Championship.

A gift of your time

Catherine Clancy

Claire (not her real name) and I have been friends for years, in fact since 1980. Of course that was back in an era when she and I had very lowly positions in the organisation for which we both worked. That friendship was maintained all through the years, seeing both of us get on the ladder that has left us both where we are today, having jobs that are exceptionally demanding, where we have little control of our own lives and where time is the enemy.

It has been like this for a number of years. We have moved from spending at least one or even two evenings a week and many weekends away together to now meeting only on very rare occasions. These meetings are prefaced by numerous cancellations and rearrangements before we actually meet.

I'm very lucky with Claire. She understands the crazy life I lead at the moment, and I understand how very busy she is. Yet I hear her speak when we eventually do get to meet about the amount of time she has spent with her many other friends, and I think to myself, Where does she get the time?

I recall three years ago when I was doing our Christmas list and I certainly was wondering when I was going to get the time to do all this shopping. Claire was on my list. I phoned her and asked her what she would like me to get her for Christmas. Her response made me think about the whole issue of managing my time and putting people first. She said she would love if she and I could spend an evening together, going out for something to eat and catching up. She wanted me to give her my time as a Christmas gift. I frantically looked at my diary for some space and almost rang her to say we would leave our

Christmas gift until after Christmas, in the new year, when I would have more time. I stopped myself.

We did meet one evening the week before Christmas, had a lovely meal and a glass of wine, and chatted for three hours. I left her thinking that I am never going to leave it so long again before making time for a really good friend, who knows me better than most.

Of course, you know the sequel to this story. I still do not meet Claire as regularly as we used to, and I still have to find time for my friend. And do you know, the longer I leave it to pick up the phone to connect with her the harder it gets.

I have reflected on how we all use our time in a highly techno-logical era and have come to realise that advances in communications systems have created barriers to us really communicating.

We have mobile phones, e-mail, internet, intranet, and we use these modern machines to create a barrier between ourselves and people. My career in the Garda Síochána has always been about people, whether it is the public I serve or the colleagues I work with: they are people. Whenever there are difficult problems to work through these are usually the result of a lack of meaningful commu-nication. E-mail and text messages convey words, but words without expression can be meaningless and can lead to misunderstandings. Why can we not pick up the phone any more and just talk?

The words 'pressure' and 'stress' are ones we are all very familiar with in modern society. Do any of us know what these words meant, say, twenty years ago? Loneliness and isolation are states of mind that are synonymous with the lives we live today. Are we as individuals responsible for causing stress, pressure, loneliness and isolation to others by our own behaviour?

I go back to the modern modes of communication, which we all use to connect with our friends, our family and our colleagues. Text messages have replaced the phone call. We use text messages to mask the guilt we feel at not having been in touch with someone. We have ful-filled our 'obligation' to keep in touch by sending the text message, then it is over to you: it is now up to you to make the next move; and the longer we engage in this frivolous, uncaring method of communicating the harder it becomes to really engage with those we love and care for.

And what of those who are in receipt of our text messages and our e-mail: how do they feel? They probably feel, and rightly so, that we are pushing them away, that we no longer care, that we are too wrapped up in our own lives to be bothered with them. What, therefore, are we creating but a society of selfish, uncaring people? What legacy are we leaving to the next generation? It is certainly not the legacy that was left to us by our parents. When our generation was growing up there was always a welcome in the home, and the kettle was always boiling. Nowadays you must make an appointment to visit, and it is less trouble to open a bottle than make the tea.

I recall the retirement function of a friend and colleague, when I was struck by the numbers of speakers who paid tribute to this man because of his ability to make time for everyone. This was something that he did so well and yet he was in a leadership position in the organisation, and his job was more pressured than most; and yet he 'made time for others.' This is how he will be remembered.

Alice talks about the casualties of an uncaring society whom she meets daily in TRUST. Is there not a danger that we could become casualties ourselves? There is a danger that, by being so casual about communicating with our friends, family and colleagues, when we retire or become ill, we will find that those people respond to us with text messages and e-mail, when we long for them to spend some time with us.

How do we, as leaders, respond to the challenge that Alice Leahy has presented us with? What can we do in our leadership positions that will begin to make a dent in the attitude that prevails in our society in relation to communication, or lack thereof? I will present the following as my contribution to the debate and to leading the change.

This Christmas, instead of racing around to buy the perfect gift for your friends and family, why not give them the gift of your time? Extend that to birthdays also.

Instead of sending a text message, just dial the number and speak.

Think about how you would like to be remembered by your family and your friends, and try to become that person.

Time is a very precious gift, which we only have on loan; use it for the enjoyment of others and you will enjoy it yourself.

Catherine Clancy, a native of Co. Donegal, is an assistant commissioner in the Garda Síochána—the first woman appointed to that rank—in charge of human resource management. She has served in Pearse Street (Dublin), Naas, the Technical Bureau, Ballyshannon, the Community Relations Section, Dungarvan, Lucan, and Letterkenny. She has also served with the United Nations Transitional Authority in Cambodia.

Rethinking time

Jean Clarke

When I'm asked to speak or write about something, I usually start by exploring the meaning of the language used to describe the subject matter. In my search for definitions of time I note that, in my edition of the *Longman Dictionary of the English Language*, there are approximately sixty-five references. That surprises me—and yet it doesn't, given that we are daily challenged with regard to the notion of time.

Most references to time are more than familiar to me, like 'ahead of one's time,' 'all in good time,' 'behind the times,' 'play for time,' 'time-killer,' 'pass the time of day,' 'time-consuming,' to mention but a few. It seems to me from this sample selection of references that the last two are most pertinent to how we might begin to look at the notion of 'wasting time with people' and how we might move beyond it.

An exploration of the word 'waste', both as a noun and a verb, is also illuminating: 'a sparsely settled, barren or devastated region,' or 'to atrophy, debilitate, emaciate or misspend.' But firstly let me start with a story.

On an October evening only days before writing this piece I was driving through the city; it was after 10 p.m. and it was dark. When stopped at traffic lights next to a hostelry in a commercial part of the city I noticed an older, frail-looking woman talking to a young man. He wore the black uniform of the hospitality trade and was smoking a cigarette. He was looking forward, out towards the passing traffic. She wore a winter jacket, was tightly holding on to her handbag and stood to his side as she spoke to him. Being shorter than he, she looked up into his face; he continued quietly to draw on his cigarette and to cast his gaze at the traffic.

In the short time I lingered at the traffic lights I wondered about this moment in time for the two people I observed. What were her origins and her needs? What were his? Of course I can only speculate. He was probably taking time off for himself, a recreational moment away from the busyness of serving drinks to others. The woman was probably looking for company, for a connection with someone, to pass the time of day (or, in this case, night) with another, albeit fleetingly. The man, it seemed, wanted time for himself; the woman appeared to need time with another person. I wondered if on his part there was ambivalence about the presence of the woman. Did she notice it? Were either aware of her vulnerability?

Needing time for self and for another and, more importantly, making this time available is, I believe, what underpins caring and what it means to care. Did the young man feel, I wonder, that he was wasting time in what looked like a time-poor moment for him, a brief escape to smoke a cigarette? Did he miss the opportunity to respond to the invitation to be present to the woman and her engagement with him? What difference would it have made to both of them had he turned his gaze away from the traffic and towards her? What would such a gaze have said to her of his being there, being present to her, even for the brief moment of his cigarette break?

Attention to another person is a fundamental principle of living, but is it possible in the absence of attention to the self? After all, being present to another might be difficult if I'm not comfortable with being present to myself, choosing instead to drift along in life's contingency of busyness. How often do we take time for 'me'—quiet time, doing-nothing time? We need this type of time to take note of what is around us, whether it is admiring the arrival of a spring flower or the movement of clouds, so that at other times we can be present to others, and to the possibility such shared moments provide for an enhanced humanity and meaning of life. This attention to time means making decisions about how we allocate our time, between the rat race and whirlpool of modernity and our need to contemplate and reflect upon the sacredness of the embodied self, its ambitions, wounds, disappointments, achievements and celebrations. The alternative is a barren, atrophied, debilitated self and society, where we are diminished by our busyness, both ourselves and others. At its most extreme this diminished state can lead to indifference and eventual disengagement. This is a vulnerable place to be in a society where there is social ambivalence about vulnerability.

So when it comes to the question of who should give leadership, I pose the question: is being present and being mindful to self and to other (or others) something someone else has to do, or is it something we all need to do? The answer is simple: leadership towards giving time to self and sharing time with other is a responsibility for each one of us. However, that is not to say that the journey will be easy; but then each journey starts with a first step. What will your first step be? A suggestion, if I may offer one, would be to acknowledge in the first place that people matter, that I matter; or, in the words of an African proverb, 'a person is a person through other persons,' or its alternative rendering, 'I am because we are; we are because I am.'

Jean Clarke is a senior lecturer in the School of Nursing, Dublin City University. Before her academic career she was a public health nurse. Her research interests include the principles of caring and presence in nursing practice and health and nursing issues in the developing world. Jean likes to spend some of her free time knitting and sewing.

Wasting time in traffic

Catherine Cleary

If I can just get to the next set of traffic lights before they change, the next road sign, past the supermarket and then round the last bend home. Every night the same rhythm. Every day the same return trip. Here is my dream home, we commuters reason. Here are my space, views, peace. The only glitch is, we have to spend three hours a day on the road to go to an office and work to pay for them.

We sleep in one county and live and work in another. We pack tired children into their car seats with breakfast in a beaker and pray to the god of commuters there is nothing up ahead that will unravel our route. One burst water main, one accident, a bulb blown in a traffic light, and flow turns to a crawl. Then it's the life of quiet desperation, all our horsepower taking us no faster than a stroll, our shoulders tensing to iron. Time dripping into the asphalt under our tyres.

The road grows into our souls. On our deathbed we will not say we wish we spent more time on the N11 or the N7 or the N-whatever. It is N for nothing. It is the in-between time, the time that (if we had the choice) we would spend differently. It is time that we might be able to spend getting to know our neighbours, if they too weren't shackled to their steering wheels. We might have more time to coach a schoolboy soccer team or man a cake stall at the school fête at the weekend if we weren't so exhausted at the end of a working week.

It's the time when those dispiriting phone calls home strain our relationships. 'Sorry, love, the traffic's grim. It's going to be another hour at least. No, there's nothing I can do. Tell him I'll read him a story tomorrow night.'

It's the time when thoughts can turn to the people who benefit from all this. We think of the developers and landowners who planted acres of greenness with bricks and mortar, without schools, work-places or public parks for the occupants to use. We think of the politicians and planners who allowed the sprawl to get out of control until a ninety-mile round-trip to the office became routine. We think of the people who leave their home at five in the morning to beat the rush and then turn and sleep cramped in the driving seat until work begins.

We think of the powers-that-be who built roads instead of railway lines, painted bus corridors onto them and then failed to put enough buses on the routes. We think of the powerful and the powerless. We feed the machine, pump the fuel and live the commuter dream.

We might think of the well-worn path that other countries have gone down, embracing the strip development and homes where life is possible only with a car. We see the hard-won lessons that others have learnt and we ignored. We see this life stretching ahead of us for ten, twenty years, every year bringing more cars onto the roads. Bigger cars. Bigger drivers, growing larger on a diet of petrol-station snacks.

And maybe we think of packing it all in, putting up the 'for sale' sign and moving to a smaller home nearer to work. We reassess our attitudes to where the best place is to rear a family. Maybe it is a smaller house or apartment with two extra hours in the day, clawed back from the road and given back to us like a gift to ourselves.

Catherine Cleary is a freelance journalist and author. She has worked as crime correspondent of the *Irish Times* and security correspondent of the *Sunday Tribune* and is the author of *Life Sentence,* a book about the families of murder victims. She is married to Liam Reid, and they have two sons.

Shop talk

Michael Clifford

They closed down in the first week of June 2007, as the summer began to blossom. John and Freda Heaslip had seen forty of those summers from behind the counter of their shop cum off-licence. John could tell you stories about how there were only six cars in the neighbourhood when they first opened for business. Nobody had very much then, and you had to work all the hours God gave you to ensure that ends were met.

New winds blew into town as the years wore on. Feargal Quinn opened up in Finglas, and in order to attract customers he sent around a bus. Then the convenience-brand market—the Spars, Maces, Centras—began to expand. Around the corner from Heaslip's a new off-licence opened up, broadening the range of alcohol on sale.

Times change. The Spar shop over the road was sold a few years ago. Now all the staff come from beyond these shores, to escape poverty in their own lands. They are polite, professional and eager to grab the opportunity to make money.

They are also transient, and unlikely to weave themselves into the fabric of the community. You won't, as they say in certain parts of the country, meet a chat too readily when you go in there. You couldn't help meeting a chat any time you wandered into Heaslip's. It was as if conversation and engagement were part of the service, and the couple were as eager to give you their time as to sell you their wares.

The changing nature of convenience shopping is as good a place as any to examine how the price of time has rocketed, and the resultant fall-out for a sense of community.

The local shop, as we know it, is fast disappearing. John and Freda were among the dwindling band of independents, certainly in Dublin.

They had time for everybody, and their establishment, like thousands of others around the country, was a focal point for the local community. Each of these shops had its own unique character. This included the proprietor, staff and physical features of the shop. Heaslip's had a large glass display case stretching the length of the counter, across which ranged all manner of edibles. You could find a bag of grapes sitting beside a plastic container of chocolate bars, next to which might be a few heads of lettuce.

Finding an unusual item might take a minute of two, during which there could be talk about local politics or sport, or an addition to the family. There was no rush. The proprietors had all the time in the world, and as the conversation grew warm you realised that spending yours in this way was an activity you could pursue with profit.

While you were waiting, somebody else might enter the shop and be drawn into the conversation. Introductions made, names put to faces, and a tiny little advance in the sense of community achieved. Nearly invariably, you left the shop feeling better than when you went in.

For some, the interaction at a local shop took on a precious quality. Those who lived alone found this an oasis in their day. The television in the corner at home was a distraction, but, lacking in human empathy, it wasn't exactly in a position to interact. Others, whose working life was spent, had time to kill and found this a pleasurable way to do so.

And then there were the people whom Alice Leahy identifies as the 'outsiders'. For them the local shop was a place where suspicion and isolation melted away. There was an opportunity to interact with those of us who lead a more conventional life. From our point of view the man or woman who might be somebody to avoid on the street could now be presented as a real person. Barriers were broken down. This person was no longer somebody to be avoided.

The contrast with our well-stocked, well laid-out chain convenience stores couldn't be more stark. In products, choice, convenience foods, we've never had it so good. We enter at pace, scan the isles and spot the product with the reassuringly familiar brand. Then hand over the cash and an eastern European smile says thank you and sends you on your way. Suits the staff, suits you. No time to talk. No time to listen. What, in any event, would you have to say?

And so, the community contracts. What was once a place of meeting is now strictly for commerce. This suits everybody. After all, the price of time has gone through the roof. It is no longer viable to waste it by talking to people.

Well, it suits nearly everybody. Those who cling to the edges of society now find that the changes in convenience shopping have been a harbinger of further isolation. The outsider now has less opportunity to engage with mainstream society. It's a small change in the greater scheme of things, but significant to lonely individuals. As a result, he or she is pushed a little bit further towards the margins.

They are not the only ones to feel this change. With time being the price it is in modern Ireland, the rest of us are fixated on spending it wisely. Time spent with people—just a few minutes here and there— seems to be a luxury few of us are willing to splash out on these days. And, ultimately, we are all the poorer for that.

Life has improved hugely for most of us living in Ireland today. For one thing, we can actually live here and don't have to emigrate. But if we have taken three steps forward we have also taken one step back. The casual interactions, each another brick in the great wall of community, are becoming more difficult to find. What was once an instinctual way of life can now be retrieved only by concerted effort, and where to start is anybody's guess.

Michael Clifford is a columnist and reporter with the *Sunday Tribune*.

Time to heal

Davis Coakley

James McCormick published an interesting and challenging book in 1979 entitled *The Doctor: Father Figure or Plumber*. In this book he argued that doctors were moving away from the compassionate and caring aspects of their profession and concentrating instead on tests and procedures, becoming in effect 'clinical plumbers'. The scientific revolution has convinced many doctors and others that scientific knowledge can provide solutions for virtually all clinical problems and challenges. The rapid growth of medical technology, which has continued apace since James McCormick published his book, has encouraged an increasing reliance on sophisticated technology to make a diagnosis. Yet, ironically, a doctor who makes time to listen attentively may narrow the list of possible diagnoses and as a result will dispense with unnecessary tests.

If a doctor is to adopt a holistic approach to his or her practice then it is very important to set time aside to listen. Most doctors in current practice work under considerable pressure, irrespective of their speciality or whether they are based in hospitals or the community. It is not easy to find longer periods that provide individuals with an opportunity to tell their story. Many general practitioners will get to know a patient over a period of years, and if the doctor is skilful he or she will know which individuals require more time. A further appointment that allows more time to listen can be arranged if necessary.

Where the doctor is working in a multi-disciplinary team there are others, such as nurses, social workers, physiotherapists and occupational therapists, who will also have opportunities to listen. An individual may talk about serious issues in his or her life to any member of the multi-disciplinary team. Valuable insights can be obtained through such encounters, which, when shared with team members, will produce a much more informed and holistic approach by the team to the individual's concerns.

Students are taught communication skills in most medical schools today. Significant stress is placed on the importance of listening for effective communication. However, such teaching will not make a lasting impact unless the students are given time to practise these skills. Students and young doctors should have the opportunity to see their senior medical teachers using listening skills effectively, both in general hospital and general practice settings. It is particularly important that they see their senior colleagues set time aside to listen to particularly vulnerable patients, such as older people, those with chronic diseases and those living in poor social conditions. Without an emphasis on the importance of listening to the concerns of individuals there is a danger that students and young doctors could mature into clinical technicians, as feared by James McCormick, with narrow perspectives and with no appreciation of the importance of setting time aside to listen.

Pressures and demands on medical schools, hospitals and general practice are constantly increasing. For instance, the efficiency of medical schools today is measured largely by their research output, rather than by the quality of their teaching. Moreover, the increasing pressures on clinical staff to see as many patients as possible leaves little time for listening and even less time to show to students effective communication in action. Yet research has shown that patients benefit when the doctor has time to listen, and also that doctors who listen get more personal satisfaction from their work.

Time is also a very important factor in developing a strong doctor-patient relationship, as this cannot occur when the doctor is rushed. If doctors are so pressured that they have little time to listen to their patients they will not get to know them, not appreciate individual preferences and wishes, nor be able to provide effective counselling and health education.

Making time to listen is not important only in directing investigations, appropriate treatment and social supports: it is also vital if the individual patient is to be treated with compassion. As James McCormick has emphasised, listening with compassion can restore 'to every man his right to human dignity.'

Davis Coakley is a consultant physician in geriatric medicine at St James's Hospital, Dublin, and professor of medical gerontology at Trinity College, Dublin. He has written and edited a number of books on medicine, the history of medicine, and literary subjects.

Glasnevin Cemetery

Mervyn Colville

Alice comes from the same town as me in Co. Tipperary, Fethard, and lived two houses down from me on the same road. My mother had told me of the work Alice was doing with the homeless, and through my work in Glasnevin our paths have crossed on many occasions. Indeed between us we have arranged a plot for the TRUST organisation in Glasnevin Cemetery. The plot is marked like any other grave here; Alice once told me that it is always a concern to those she meets to blend in with 'normal' people and not to be treated differently.

I come from a rural background, where the funeral director knows the family; everyone knows the priest and the gravediggers. Initially the most striking aspect of my job (besides working in a graveyard) was how big the death business is in the big city. We bury and cremate more than three thousand persons every year—not to mention the thousands who visit graves regularly, those who attend our various masses each year for those interred, including our cemetery mass and our angels mass for babies.

Many people come to the office wishing to find their loved ones. They've forgotten the grave, although they know it's 'by a tree'! Many people have said to me, 'I don't remember how we got to the cemetery on the morning of the funeral, never mind finding the grave from memory.' We get to meet many people at their lowest ebb, and trying to deal with them in a sensitive manner is always difficult. It is a constant struggle to individualise the attention we give to people when they come to our cemeteries and crematoria. Trying to cater for ten to fifteen interments and cremations daily and give each of those families the time and compassion they deserve at such a terrible time is one of our biggest challenges.

Time, of course, is never wasted with people on these occasions. In fact, if anything, contact with people who have lost a loved one brings home very powerfully just how much time we fail to waste with others and maybe only realise that when they are gone.

The 'we' I refer to is Glasnevin Cemeteries Group, of which I am the manager. Glasnevin Cemetery, the largest cemetery in Ireland, opened its gates in 1832 after Daniel O'Connell formed a committee to administer the cemetery to allow both Catholics and Protestants to be buried in a dignified manner. Prospect Cemetery, as it is now known, has grown from 9 acres to more than 120 acres. Approximately 1½ million men, women and children are laid to rest here. Many famous people are interred in Glasnevin: Ann Devlin, Maud Gonne MacBride, Margaret Burke Sheridan, Daniel O'Connell, Michael Collins, Éamon de Valera, Brendan Behan, Charles Stewart Parnell, Luke Kelly, to name but a few.

But many of those 1½ million souls are buried in what we term 'unmarked' graves. There were many reasons for this, mostly financial. Incidentally, Charles Stewart Parnell chose to be buried with the poor of Dublin.

A vast number of burials in Glasnevin took place during the epidemics—cholera and smallpox—and the Famine; and, as the records show, there was no attendance at the graveside. Fortunately, we have records of every person interred in the cemetery, and the information taken is standard for all the burials, both in purchased family graves and communal graves, which makes for easy retrieval, and therefore no-one is forgotten.

Our records date from 1828 and are divided into 'General Ground' and 'Poor Ground' registers. Thankfully, the term 'Poor Ground' is no longer used today. It clearly portrays the divide that existed between those who have and those who have not. Many interred may have been financially poor but were rich in many other ways, one example being Michael Moran or Zozimus (1794–1846), the balladeer, also known as the Blind Bard of the Liberties. He was born in Dublin and lived there all his life. At two weeks old he was blinded by illness. He made his living reciting verses that he composed in his own lively if semi-literate manner. Some of them still survive, such as 'Saint Patrick was a Gentleman' and 'The Finding of Moses'.

Another person interred, and one well known to TRUST, is Johnny, whose grave is marked by a simple wooden cross made by another man known to TRUST. I was contacted by Alice to find the grave. We tidied it up, and when Alice arrived to place the cross on it she was happy to see that Johnny was buried under a tree, as he had a great love for nature and slept out for a lot of his adult life.

John Keegan from Shanahoe, Co. Laois, is also buried in Glasnevin. He died in the cholera sheds of the poorhouse, now St James's Hospital. His most famous poem is 'Pinch and Caoch Ó Laoire'. I had a meeting at his graveside with Donncha Ó Dúlaing, Alice, Tony Delaney and some friends. Tony has collected the works of John Keegan and, with others, has placed a headstone on his unmarked grave.

Time spent focused on others, even after they have passed away, can help us. In celebrating their achievements in the cemetery we remind ourselves of the good they did, how they tried to help others, the works they have left us that also make our lives a little better, if only to lift our spirits. More importantly, however, that time may inspire us to make a little bit more effort for others.

Mervyn Colville, a native of Co. Tipperary, is manager of Glasnevin Cemeteries Group.

Personal service

Louis Copeland

I started out in the business when I was about ten years old. I would go in to my dad after school and run messages for him. His name was Louis too. I'm a grandfather now, and I've a son Louis and a grandson Louis.

Back in those days things were tough. They were not as good as they are now, but Dublin was a much more friendly place. It wasn't as busy, and with not as many people you found the people had more time to look out for each other.

Tailoring was all my father knew. He was never really a business-man; he was more of a tradesman, I suppose. In those days people didn't plan. Nowadays it's all about looking ahead and thinking about opportunities.

If staff are happy where they work, that translates into customers being happy. Taking time with people makes it more personal. I love when I see a man bringing a wife or partner in with him, because they'll spend more and be more adventurous with their colours.

I suppose people buy suits for a lot of reasons. You have business suits and occasion suits, like weddings. When I'm dealing with people I'll always try and find out what they want and what they do. If you have someone who will only have one suit you don't want anything too pronounced. Although men's fashion is different from women's, you do have the changes every six months or so. Lapels get wider or the stripes get louder.

We deal with everyone, from workers in the street to Supreme Court judges. You have to approach people in different ways, and every customer is an individual. Some people can be very talkative when you're measuring them, and you get to hear about their lives.

There is a trust in the relationship between a man and his tailor. I can keep secrets. I've heard many over the years.

You get some very nice people, and sometimes you might wish that everybody could be that nice. Lots of my high-profile customers like to be treated as if they're ordinary; and then there are a few people who expect the red-carpet treatment.

Although we have all the modern technology, like e-mail and internet, there is nothing to beat lifting the phone and talking to someone. You can interpret what's going on so much more easily and get a vibe from someone that you just won't get through a text or e-mail. We hope our customers turn off their mobile phones when they come in and get a bit of peace. It is that personal touch that keeps people coming back.

The shop has always been in Capel Street, although the building has changed. You get a great mix of people here, from the Four Courts to the Bridewell and the Fruit Market. I usually say that Capel Street is a destination shop. People make the effort to come here—not like Grafton Street, where there is a passing trade.

Dealing with everyone in a friendly manner is what makes the difference. In all areas of life I've found that you get back what you put in.

Louis Copeland, a native of Dublin, is a well-known tailor and businessman and a trustee of TRUST. The Copeland family have been in the tailoring business in Dublin for a hundred years.

The art of greeting

Jarlath Daly

L ife in a provincial town in the 60s and 70s was, in hindsight, an idyllic place. The pace of everyday living was easygoing and safe. It was a time of trust and neighbourly interaction. Doors were open and problems were solved with help from next door or around the corner. People greeted one other, had a chat and just made time for each other. 'A problem shared is a problem halved.'

Contemporary Ireland presents a different experience altogether. In city, suburbia and dormitory towns, the concept of community is almost a thing of the past. We know bus, train and Luas timetables; the cost of mortgages, new cars and the rising cost of everyday commodities are the topic of the day. Isolation and consumerism result in the lack of investment of time in people. 'We know the price of everything but the value of nothing.'

With the advent of technology the demise of conversation began, and its art is now confined to the scrapheap. Collecting the messages years ago involved a walk to the local shop, having a chat and home again. Today's 'messages' are held in your mobile phone.

There are many advantages of modern technology—let's not go back to the Stone Age; but there are also disadvantages. Because of the pressures of modern society, work loads, commuting and peer pressure, community spirit is on the bottom rung of the ladder. Early daily departures and late home arrivals leave communities bereft of human interaction. Knowledge of our neighbours' successes or failures, joys or sorrows go unknown to us. Everyone's head is buried in the sand, oblivious of the problems others may have.

It is these problems that grow like a cancer and create the 'rejected' or disenfranchised in society today. Do we have the capacity to respond to change? It is incumbent on us all to value the individuality of every-one in this 21st-century multicultural Ireland. Let's take time and revive the art of greeting, thus encouraging the value and respect for all. If one caring word or smile can prevent another from being excluded, we may see the rebirth of a caring Ireland.

As Canon John Hayes of Muintir na Tíre said, 'better to light a candle than curse the darkness.'

Jarlath Daly is a sculptor. A native of Co. Tipperary, he is well known for his enthusiasm for rugby and the GAA and is a former president of the Tipperary Association in Dublin.

The storyteller

Tony Delaney

One evening last winter—a holiday evening too—when the western wind was sweeping on wild pinions from the grey hills of Tipperary, athwart the rich and level plains of the Queen's County, when the blast roared down in the chimney, and the huge rain-drops pattered saucily against the four tiny panes which constituted the little kitchen window, I was sitting in the cottage of a neighbouring peasant, amid a small but happy group of village rustics, and enjoying with them that enlivening mirth and sinless delight which I have never found anywhere but at the fireside of an Irish peasant. The earthen floor was well scrubbed over, the 'brullaws of furniture' were arranged with more than usual tidiness, and even the crockery on the well-scoured dresser reflected the ruddy glare of the red fire with redoubled brilliancy, and glittered and glistened as merrily as if they felt conscious of the calm and tranquility of that happy scene. And happy indeed was that scene, and happy was that time, and happier still the hearts of the laughing rustics by whom I was on that occasion surrounded, and amongst whom I have spent the lightest and happiest hours of my existence. The songs of our sires, chanted with all that melancholy softness and pathetic sweetness for which the voices of our wild Irish girls are remarkable, the wild legend recited with that rich brogue and waggish humour peculiar alone to the Irish peasant, and the romantic and absurd fairy tale, told with all the reverential awe and caution which the solemnity of the subject required, long amused and excited the captivated auditors.

When John Keegan, poet, writer and storyteller, wrote these lines deep in the winter of 1841 near Shanahoe, Co. Laois, Ireland under the rule of Queen Victoria was a different place. It is said that the past is a foreign country, and certainly pre-Famine Ireland, with mud-walled cabins dotting the rural landscape, seems a distant place. And yet the peasantry, as Keegan depicts, were happy in their simplicity. It was a time of storytelling, banshees, raths and changelings.

Keegan's literary talent thrived in a fertile storytelling landscape. The stories were all around him in the nightly ramblings to the cabins of his neighbours. It was a time of talking, a time of 'rambling,' a time of caring, a time of neighbourliness. Keegan's pen captured it all for future generations to relish and to reflect upon.

I was born in Keegan's village of Shanahoe in the mid-1960s, and 'rambling' was still a popular night-time pastime for my father and for his generation in the early years of my childhood, though it was struggling hard to overcome the threat of television. I well remember the houses of the village where the rambling tradition prospered. The owner of one such house had refused to accept electricity, despite the best efforts of rural electrification; and yet that house, with its half-door, was crowded by night, winter and summer alike, with ramblers spending time, talking time, being together.

Today the rambling-houses of the village, just like the ramblers and the half-doors, have all passed away. Modern life-styles, appliances and technology have replaced the rich rambling tradition of Ireland's past. Ireland has changed in the name of progress. Perhaps it is a better place economically. Is it a happier place? Would John Keegan 'fit in' to the modern Irish life-style, or is the person who enjoys a simple life an outsider? Who will tell the story of our generation?

I wonder what Keegan, the storyteller, would make of it all.

> Oh! God be with those happy times,
> Oh! God be with my childhood,
> When I, bare-headed, roamed all day
> Bird-nesting in the wild-wood—
> I'll not forget those sunny hours,
> However years may vary;
> I'll not forget my early friends,
> Nor honest Caoch O'Leary.

Tony Delaney joined the civil service in 1985 and has worked in a number of departments. He is now an assistant commissioner in the Office of the Data Protection Commissioner. One of the leading authorities on the life and works of the nineteenth-century writer John Keegan, he edited *John Keegan: Selected Works* (1997) and in 1999 founded the John Keegan School. He was involved in the raising of a monument on Keegan's grave in Glasnevin Cemetery, Dublin, to commemorate the 150th anniversary of his death. He is also joint editor (with Pádraig Ó Macháin) of *Like Sun Gone Down: Selections from the Writings of John Canon O'Hanlon* (2005).

Time to walk

Susan Gageby Denham

In Ireland we are losing the time to walk, and with it valuable aspects of society. Time is eaten up in the car, driving, queuing, stewing, in hurried haste, stationary, frantic, folly. The loss diminishes the community, whether it be rural or urban.

As we walk along beside the drystone wall a wren wings out to inspect the intruders. He stands sentry until we pass, tail up, beady eye, sounding the alarm. The lark dips and trills above our heads. Across the bay the cuckoo is calling. The fuchsia is budding, promising a rosy future.

The walk is purposeful, to buy milk and other staples at the local shop. As the road rises we meet John. We discuss the weather, the state of the land—flooded—and his children in New York. Well past three score years and ten, he lives a full life, albeit without his beloved spouse these last two years. By the lake we note the level of the water and smell newly varnished boats. Paintbrush in hand, our neighbour brings us up to date on local events.

The shop is dry and warm. Full of lingering people. No haste. No trolleys. It is a hub for the community and dispenses news, advice and groceries.

A walk in the city is equally rich. Walking through the legal quarter in Dublin, there is a confirmation of the old and new. The smell signals the retreating tide, a sniffy Liffey—a very different riverscape from full tide, when grey mullet congregate below the bridge. Walking near the Four Courts early in the morning, I look forward to meeting the lady with the trolley who feeds the local cats, wild and domestic, on a weedy corner. We discuss the mewing and preening cats, especially the little black-and-white kitten, which is growing stronger. A group of cool dudes slouch by on their way to Franciscan support. Darkly suited young lawyers hurry by, clutching paper files, deep in conversation.

The salty smell of the Fish Market is gone. Many a fine dinner was bought here. The women traders, who spent their working lives at scaly, glistening tables laid out with fruits of the sea, enriched the lives of their customers. However, the forklifts rattle over the cobbles in the Fruit and Vegetable Market. Laconic exchanges ring through the air, laced with Dublin wit. The bustle commenced before dawn and is well established. The smell of coffee and fresh bread wafts from modern cafés and shops, drawing in the early risers for cappuccino and croissants. Children of the New Ireland walk through the streets to school. This ancient part of Dublin has welcomed waves of people who have swept up on its shore over thousands of years.

The legal quarter is changing; new developments tower over artisan streets. The grand buildings housing courts and legal centres of learning, both old and new, create a foundation in the area. The horse-drawn carts, hay and oats, of Smithfield have given way to new communities: a series of villages in the city, developing their own spirit; a place to find time to walk.

In Ireland, a land where the pace of life has quickened, it is often difficult to find time to walk. Recently it was argued by Chris Goodall that if you wish to live a low-carbon life it may make more sense to drive a car than walk, if walking means you need to eat more, to replace the energy lost. However, he did not intend to recommend the car. Rather, he was presenting a case that modern food production is an important and under-recognised source of climate-changing gases. Whether one accepts his argument or not, it represents a view on the globalisation of food production. The fact that vegetables come from the Near East, fruit from Africa and chicken from the Far East should not deter further our decision to walk.

Global trade decisions ultimately reverberate through our villages, rural and urban. However, rather than endorse and support the leaching of local life, with all its inherent supportive strength, whenever possible, find time to walk.

Time to walk is much more than merely using Shanks's mare. The oldest form of transport, it carries with it communication and community. People and places do not flash past in a swish of tyres and a beat of a tune, heading to a virtual world. Rather, the web of the community, so fragile, is woven and strengthened with our steps.

Susan Gageby Denham became the first woman appointed to the Supreme Court in December 1992. She has been a member of the Courts Service Board since it was established and chaired the board from 2001 to 2004. In 2006 the Government established the Working Group on a Court of Appeal, which she chairs. She is also a bencher of the Honorable Society of King's Inns, an honorary bencher of the Middle Temple, London, Pro-Chancellor of the University of Dublin, and president of the University of Dublin Law Society. She is married to Dr Brian Denham, and they have four grown-up children.

The watch from Istanbul

Rev. Olive Donohoe

Istanbul—Constantinople—Byzantium. That's where I came to understand what a necessary and wonderful thing it is to waste time with people. It happened like this.

I was lucky enough to be able to do one of the pastoral training placements with the Anglican Chaplaincy in Istanbul one summer in the late 1990s. At the time I was an ordinand in the Church of Ireland Theological College, Dublin. The chaplain, the Rev. (now Canon) Ian Sherwood, was an old college friend and happily had agreed to offer me a pastoral placement. I was to become part of the everyday church life and participate in the various ministries of the chaplaincy. Along with the other Christian churches in Istanbul, the Anglican Church was part of a programme for helping and supporting refugees and economic migrants. The population of the city had increased by almost two million in as many years.

During and following the Gulf War in the 1990s many of the non-national Kuwaitis were forced to leave Kuwait. This exodus, and the many horrendous tragedies of drought, war and famine in Africa, made Istanbul a gathering-place for many who were seeking refuge, safety, or new life. Of course one has only to look at a map of Turkey to see why: it was a natural geographical springboard for Europe and longed-for safety.

The Refugee and Economic Migrant Programme was a particular, local Christian response to the increasing number of people seeking help at the various church doors in Istanbul. In an attempt to make myself useful I joined in teaching the children of the refugees and migrants in a tiny school the Anglican congregation had set up in the back of their church. These people were officially non-existent in Turkey and unable to go to local schools.

Being part of that little school at the back of the church was great fun. I had never taught before and really enjoyed it. These children had endured a lot in their short lives, and school was really wonderful for them. And then a short course was established to help the adult refugees and migrants learn and improve their English.

The weather in Istanbul that summer was very hot, so I never wore a watch. The adult language sessions were relatively short—an hour or so at a time. A knowledge of English meant that they might have a chance of some kind of future, as they would be more likely to be accepted by English-speaking countries if they were eventually accepted into the official UN refugee programme. And so, in order to give them plenty of opportunities to speak English, each time I met one of them around the church or the parsonage I would politely greet them, 'Good morning, Sathees, and how are you?' And they would reply, overcoming great shyness in some cases, 'Oh, teacher, I am fine. And how are you?' And as the lessons progressed, so did our conversations.

'Good morning, Ragou, and how are you today?'

'I am very fine, teacher. And how are you?'

'I am fine, thank you. And what time is it, please?'

'Oh, teacher, it is ten o'clock.' And so it went on.

'Oh, teacher, it is lunch time.'

I always began with a greeting and then asked the time, and finally moved on to the weather. Not particularly exciting stuff, you might think, but over the weeks of meeting and greeting after classes and all through the day, most of them knew how to say the time in English, and how to talk about the weather—essential code for anyone hoping to go to an English-speaking country.

'And what time is it, please?'

'It is five o'clock, teacher.'

And so time passed, and then it was time for me to leave. I was very sad at the thought of going home and leaving them all behind. But there was a going-away party for me, complete with a presentation, which was a bit unexpected, as there was so little money around. I was really touched and opened my present there and then.

Father Ian, some members of the congregation and some of the refugees who were staying in the crypt of the church and who had faithfully attended the English classes all crowded around. The first present I opened was a lovely glass decanter, and along with this, from the refugees themselves, there was . . . a watch.

'Now, teacher, you won't have to ask us the time any more. Now you have a watch of your own.'

They had given me not only a watch, they had given me a gift of time: their time. They had listened to me, they had 'wasted' their time with me. Wasting time with people . . . ? Yes, you could say I wasted time with people too, that summer in Istanbul! And I've been wasting time with people ever since.

Rev. Olive Donohoe was born in Dublin in 1958. She trained as a certified accountant before entering the Church of Ireland Theological College in Dublin in the early 1990s. She was ordained in 1994 and served in Bandon before becoming rector of the Mountmellick Group of Parishes in Co. Laois in 1998. She is honorary treasurer of the Church of Ireland's Aid and Development Programme and the Bishops' Appeal and director of adult education in the Diocese of Meath and Kildare. She is involved in awareness-raising and debate on important issues facing both church and society today.

All time is not the same time

Theo Dorgan

She wasn't begging, not exactly.
Just sitting out of the flow.

She wasn't sitting, not exactly.
She was just there, out of the flow.

I wasn't hurrying, not exactly.
Just walking, going with the flow.

Well, not just walking,
I was worrying my way through the flow.

She looked up, and smiled.
Just that, she smiled.

and I smiled back.
Of course I did.

I reached in my pocket
but she shook her head,

she held my eyes
and let her look fall,

out of the hurting world,
out of the flow.

Theo Dorgan is a poet, broadcaster and author. His most recent publications are *Sailing for Home* (2004), *Songs of Earth and Light* (translations of Barbara Korun, 2005) and *A Book of Uncommon Prayer* (2007). He is a member of Aosdána.

Come on, let's waste it!

Bishop Walton Empey

Many years ago a fellow-bishop gave me a copy of a church magazine in which there was an article that struck me forcibly. It was written by one of our clergy in the United States, telling the reader about an episode in his life.

He had been invited back to a parish of which he was the first priest some twenty years before and was now celebrating its anniversary. As he travelled he thought of all the big plans he and his parishioners had for the new parish; all the organisations they had started; the building programmes; the money-raising and indeed all that went into the setting up of a new community.

On arrival he met many people whom he had served and was received warmly. To his surprise, none of them mentioned any of the big plans, and when he brought the subject up he was met with glazed eyes or vague memories. However, time and time again individuals spoke to him warmly about such things as his presence with them at the baptism of their first child, his ministry to them when they were sick, bereaved or lonely, the time spent visiting them in their homes and simply talking to them. In other words, it was not the big plans they recalled but the times he wasted with them: that was something they would never forget.

Like Martha in the Gospels, we clergy can be busy about many things, neglecting those that are of most importance. Jesus is the icon for all Christian ministry. He had an extraordinarily busy three years of public ministry, frequently surrounded by crowds of people and engaged in much controversy. Yet amidst all this He always seemed to have time to engage with individuals. We read of Him spending time with a leper, a blind man, Levi, Zacchaeus, a widow, a pharisee in his home, a woman suffering from a haemorrhage, a centurion, Martha and Mary and many, many others. He wasted much time with people and in doing that set a headline for all his followers.

He drives this lesson home in his teaching about the last judgement, when he blesses those who 'when I was hungry gave me food, thirsty something to drink, a stranger and you welcomed me, naked and you gave me clothing, sick and you took care of me, in prison you visited me.' Could the challenge be clearer?

Contributors to this book were asked the question, Who should give leadership in making our society a more welcoming place? The churches must play their part in this matter, for that is clearly their calling. To be fair, many parishes and individual Christians are already committed. I see that happening in many places throughout the country. Busy people always seem to find time if directly challenged, which has been my experience throughout my ministry. Much is being done, but much remains to be done. All of us, clergy and lay, are given the challenge and the responsibility of wasting time with people.

Of course, such an attitude is not only confined to Christians but also to others of different faiths or none. All of us share a common humanity, and that fact alone should be sufficient to challenge us. I believe that to waste time with people is an essential part of being human. Come on, let's waste it!

Bishop Walton Empey, former Archbishop of Dublin, is a native of Dublin. He now lives in Co. Carlow with his wife, Louisa, and has three sons and a daughter.

The Greeter

Bernard Farrell

Laguna in California is renowned for many things. Internationally, it is the setting for television glamour, series such as 'The oc' and 'Laguna Beach'—stories about wealthy young people falling in and out of love on sun-soaked sands or moon-lit beaches. Nationally, it is a favoured resort for Americans from northern California or the Mid-West states. For me it is the Laguna Playhouse, one of the oldest theatres on the West Coast, where many of my plays had their American premiere. And it was on one of my many visits to that theatre that I heard about a man who probably gave more to Laguna than most.

He was a drifter, a stranger who one day appeared in Laguna and soon became a legend in the town, known to all as 'the Greeter'.

Like many homeless, rootless people, the details of his early life are very sketchy indeed. Born in 1890, his real name was Eiler Larsen, a native of Denmark, and in the 1930s he was living rough in Washington. Then he drifted west, to San Francisco, before moving further south to Carmel and eventually on to Laguna. There he lived for the next forty years—and became famous for standing on the same street corner every day and, as his name suggests, greeting people, speaking to them, wishing them well and making them smile.

He asked for no money, no food, nothing in return. He survived on the generosity of Lagunaites, mostly in exchange for any garden-ing jobs he could do. But he spent most of his days welcoming people and engaging them in conversation. All he seemed to need in life was that people engage briefly with him, exchange a greeting, give him a little of their time before going on their way or back to their daily routine.

As his reputation grew it was discovered that what he was doing in Laguna was merely a continuation of what he had done in Carmel, in San Francisco and in Washington, where, in the dark days of the Depression, he brightened the lives of people facing financial ruin, absolute poverty and broken lives. And in all these places people came to know him very well without knowing very much about him.

Photographs taken of him in Laguna show him to be a tall, craggy-faced, long-haired, bearded man, walking the beach or sitting on park benches or, as he did every day, standing on the corner of Pacific Coast Highway and Forest Avenue, waving to passing cars or engaging pedestrians in close conversation. The wide-brimmed straw hat that sheltered him from the Californian sun also, in many photographs, hid his features from the camera . . . except on those occasions when he was throwing his head back and broadly smiling, delighting in the interaction and the conversation.

Sceptics—as ever—sometimes viewed his attitude and his behaviour with suspicion. Did he have an agenda, a reason, a motive? Did he have a past, was he on the run from something or someone, was it all a cover-up for something darker and more sinister—or was he just some crazy guy, out of his mind, smiling and greeting a world that he no longer knew anything about?

The truth, it seems, was far simpler and yet more complex. Eiler Larsen was indeed a simple man, but a man of great intelligence. He spoke six languages, was an avid reader and particularly loved the work of the New York left-wing poet Louis Untermeyer. Perhaps he had a troubled past of unrealised ambition—he certainly had very few possessions—but he did have time on his hands and he generously gave it to everyone, in the only way he knew: by greeting and meeting and only desiring a little time in return.

And I am glad to say that Laguna gave him that, and more. In 1963 the city fathers proclaimed him the Official Laguna Greeter. They gave him lifelong accommodation at the Laguna Hotel, they encased his footprints in the concrete for posterity, and after his death in 1979 they erected not one but two statues to his memory.

And today he is still lovingly cherished as the gentle man who came to Laguna with nothing to give but time. And by giving it generously he enriched this wealthy Californian town in ways that will be remembered long after the glitter of its television image has finally faded away.

Bernard Farrell is an award-winning playwright whose work is mainly premiered at the Abbey Theatre, Gate Theatre and Red Kettle Theatre and is seen extensively abroad.

Value the person

Sister Consilio Fitzgerald

I was born and reared on a farm, one of a large family. Looking back, my lasting impression as a child is one of love. I just accepted this as normal. Little I knew of the hard work and sense of purpose that goes into creating an environment within which the individual feels respected, loved, and 'at home'. This is especially the case for young people, whose impressions are formed at a very early stage, as well as those who are particularly vulnerable. We all need 'space' within which we can begin to learn (or relearn) that we are *worth* loving. As day follows night, we can then begin to reciprocate this love.

Our home, the heart of the family, was always busy. There were always jobs to be done. Work served a worthwhile purpose, of building our home and supporting the growth of the family. Work never displaced family life. This is something that, I believe, we have to think seriously about in today's world.

Time is precious. There were always jobs to be done on a farm. In the kitchen I learnt much from watching, and simply being with, my mother. I can see, looking back, that the sense and security of her presence contributed enormously to making sense of what life is about and how full it is of possibilities for good. I could see the real goodness and value in the time she made available for each one of us, despite all that had to be done, not alone for her family but for all who came to our door.

The day was always full. But, busy as it was, when the evening came, 'time' took on a different meaning. It became a 'space' for fun, sharing secrets and listening. It became a space within which we prayed, as a family. It was this that brought about the togetherness that actually made us a family. The Rosary was that moment in which a whole stream of activities of the day stopped and we were brought together. It was the same, of course, for many families in Ireland.

All of this kept us together, even when, later on, each of us embarked on our own lives. This sense of togetherness and also of suffering (because, like everyone, we had our share) were the foundations on which our family developed and our young lives built, day by day.

Today, every Cuan Mhuire—which are hives of activity during the day—comes together in the evening to create that 'space' within which we meet God, and his Mother, in praying the Rosary. This builds the sense of togetherness, and of the value of looking out for each other, that is at the centre of the Cuan Mhuire family. It is my experience, for well over forty years now, that prayer is the essential foundation for healing and is at the very heart of all the different dimensions—physical, emotional, psychological—that can make us into the persons that we were created by God to be.

What now strikes me so clearly is that by putting God first, everything else that is of importance gets done. Prayer means not just being on your knees but also up and doing whatever it is that God requires of us at this *particular* moment. It opens our eyes to see, through the help of Mary, his Mother, that each person we meet is made in the image and likeness of God: whatever their appearance, or behaviour, their lives have a unique and unrepeatable value. The truth is that without prayer it is so easy to marginalise those for whom we see no use, or whom we presume to judge. Prayer opens the door that welcomes them (because it has to come from within us) into our lives.

President Mary McAleese, a truly great leader—and a wife and mother—has wisely observed that addiction, which was an affliction to previous generations, now threatens this present generation. I see the truth of this every day—not just in the statistics (which are tragic) but in the courts and in the hurt of the growing number of individuals who come to Cuan Mhuire. Those suffering from addiction are as often as not suffering from a lack of healing in their lives. This is made much worse by the alienation they feel from family and home and from a society that simply doesn't take the time to listen—and to acknowledge not just their pain but their innate dignity and infinite worth.

I do not believe that any of us has an 'answer' to the problems of addiction and homelessness—with all that this entails—which are so closely intertwined. More laws and regulations and 'red tape' are not the answer: they are, as often as not, simply a way of 'passing the buck.' It is *our* personal responsibility, and, if we only knew it, our privilege, to make ourselves available so as to allow God to work through us. The sometimes unspeakable suffering involved in addiction truly can—and I have seen this—be enormously redemptive if only the individual person feels that there is somebody there for them and someone to walk with them on a path to recovery—as often as not one that they themselves have travelled.

This means accepting such a responsibility for all our brothers and sisters—without any exception—who are suffering from addiction and its consequences, or who have been otherwise pushed aside in the reckless pursuit by today's society of the false gods of power of one kind or another. The opportunities are there in our own lives, in our families and our places of work. It means creating the 'space' to welcome all who are marginalised into our lives. In Cuan Mhuire, with the help of our Blessed Lady, we have tried to create this sacred space. All are welcome.

Sister Consilio Fitzgerald, a native of Co. Kerry, founded Cuan Mhuire in 1966 in the Mercy Convent, Athy, Co. Kildare, now with communities in Limerick, Galway, Dublin, Tipperary, Cork, Monaghan and Newry. Cuan Mhuire provides standard-setting facilities encompassing detox, training and rehabilitation programmes for all suffering from addictions and their consequences as well as step-down transition houses and after-care programmes for the continuous support of individuals and their families. Sister Consilio has received numerous professional and civic awards in recognition of her work.

Return to sender

Gerard Mannix Flynn

There are others now packing,
Cramming mementoes into obese suitcases.
They are looking for a new life, a new beginning, a job, a few euro.
Family men and women, young boys and girls, children.
They are coming, but they will not be welcomed
The only people pleased to see them will be their traffickers.
They will be stuffed like squashed grapes into a vat. The airtight
Container will wrap around them like a monster's mouth
There will be no light for days, they will not see the ocean nor
Hear the seagulls.
To them, in the darkness, Dublin will indeed be a heaven. Grafton
Street, a wonderland
They will not experience Joyce's swerve of shore nor bend of bay,
Nor see the environs
These are the ghost people, the invisible.
Sshhh . . . can you hear them?
Fate holds them together huddled in the hold of a ship,
They are the recycled, the turned away. Fodder,
Raw product for the only industry they have ever known,
Human cargo, they are the smuggled goods.
The media will call them non-nationals, eastern Europeans,
Africans, aliens, refugees, migrants, asylum seekers, spongers . . .
But I know them as Lithuanians, Bosnians, Romanians, Nigerians
Sudanese, Irish, Russians . . . my fellows,
God knows them as his children as they are all arrested at the
Point of entry on East Wall.
God and Beckett think, 'try harder, try again.' God loves a trier.

We all love a doer.
They will now be escorted, frogmarched, corralled onto chartered
Flights
Against their bill of rights. No mention of the UN convention,
Against their will, and God's, they will be strapped in for take off,
Taken away.
The throw-away people—for export, for deport, always on the go,
On the lookout for a resting place, a halting site,
For them it will be return, return, return to sender, no address
Known
No passport, no ID papers to call their own, destination unknown
They will tell of Irish eyes not smiling
The only people pleased to see them will be their traffickers.
They are the goods in transit.
Welcome aboard flight EU two zero zero eight,
These people are not the movers and the shakers,
They are the moved on, the shaken—to their very core
Nothing to greet them but the cold, cold reception.
They are the no paid, the constantly conveyor-belted,
From port to port, land-strip to land-strip,
From detention centre to detention centre,
Prison to prison, horror to horror.
Passed on and over, over a lifetime,
Like a well-palmed coin, always in motion.
In their hearts, hope against hope rides shotgun, all they seek
Is a living
God blows his warm breath on them at 30,000 feet above, in a
Tin can they travel.
The captain announces that today they all travel first class,
But nobody understands his language, everybody prays to the
God of their choice
For one last chance, for another go at the wall, at the frontiers,
At the gates, at the borders.
God says yes, the EU says no
We all would like another chance
But the only happy smiling faces that will greet them will be
Their traffickers, their smugglers, their slave-makers
And the media, the media will call them non-nationals,
Foreigners, no-gooders, aliens,

The media will call them spongers, wasters, layabouts, criminals,
Dirt, law-breakers, moochers, job robbers but I know them as my
Friends.
I know them as my neighbours.
I know them as my brothers and my sisters.
I know them as my fellow human beings.

Gerard Mannix Flynn, born in Dublin in 1957, is a writer, actor and visual
artist. His work has garnered much critical acclaim and many awards. In 2003,
in recognition of his work, he was made a member of Aosdána. In addition to
being a working artist he sits on the board of the Irish Museum of Modern
Art, to which he was appointed by the Minister with Responsibility for the
Arts.

Today

Tony Gill

Today I spoke to no one,
And nobody spoke to me.
   Am I dead?

Tony Gill was a poet who was homeless and well known to all in TRUST. He died in 2004 and is buried in the TRUST plot in Glasnevin Cemetery, Dublin. His poems were edited by Thomas Crilly and published in *Tony Gill, Street Poet* (2006).

Two wise men

Maurice Guéret

The entrance hall at TRUST is a lovely room to meet people in. One Wednesday lunchtime in December 2006 we were about to have our monthly board meeting there when one of our dearest friends, Eddie, was about to let himself out. He looked a million dollars in his Crombie coat, having had his daily shower, shave and change of clothes.

I took the opportunity to introduce Eddie to James, our chairman at TRUST, and the two men smiled, shook hands, and wished each other well. Nine months later, as I write this piece, Eddie and James are no longer with us. James passed away at home just a few weeks after that board meeting, and in August of this year we lost Eddie to cancer in Our Lady's Hospice in Harold's Cross. They were two extraordinary men—as Éamonn Mac Thomáis used to say, professors in the University of Conversation.

James was first and foremost a family doctor: one obituary described him as the architect of modern general practice in Ireland. He abhorred the old dispensary system, where poor patients were treated in Dickensian clinics run by the state while private patients were invited into the doctor's parlour for after-hours consultations. James was elected chairman of the old Eastern Health Board (a rare achievement for somebody who was not a party hack) and he was instrumental in reforming this blight on Irish general practice.

I first came to know James as one of my professors in Trinity College Medical School, and it was clear to anybody who attended his lectures that he was very much more than a disease merchant. He spoke about people, not about their symptoms. He spoke about their needs, rather than their tablets. He spoke about the fears of patients, rather than the fears of medical practitioners. One of his greatest regrets about the state of modern health care was that doctors were so slow to recognise their own limitations.

Together with his Trinity colleague Professor Petr Skrabanek, James set out to challenge all sorts of medical orthodoxy. When pompous doctors made pronouncements, James and Petr were first to stand in line and ask for proof. All too often it was not forthcoming. They read widely and published many books between them. They challenged some of the lifelong labels doctors stuck on patients, particularly in the field of psychiatry. They poured icy-cold water on those who claimed to specialise in 'preventing illness'. They asked why doctors were so sensitive to professional criticism and independent appraisal when this was what they themselves should have been trained to do.

James had a particular warmth and empathy for those who were 'different' and channelled his steadfast principles of freedom of expression and tolerance through his work at TRUST. He accepted you as you were, and saw the role of a doctor as one who should offer comfort and friendship above all else.

Eddie was a true character who touched the lives of many in his native city. He probably knew more people in Dublin than the rest of us in TRUST put together, yet despite having so many friends and acquaintances he felt removed and apart from his people. His first job as a teenager was in an abattoir—something that must have been very hard for somebody who loved, cared for and confided in animals. He married young and had two fine children, of whom he was very proud. Later he worked in maintenance for Dublin Corporation; at one stage he held down two jobs to sustain his young family. Through no fault of his own, Eddie succumbed to mental illness and spent much of his thirties and forties in psychiatric hospitals—often against his will. His doctors might have described him as difficult to treat; Eddie saw it differently. He wanted to talk—but he found it hard to get anyone to listen. Instead he was offered tablets; when he refused he was forcibly held down for injections. He used to say, 'They know all about tablets but nothing about the mind; they don't know how I feel.'

When medication didn't work, Eddie was sent for electro-convulsive treatment. He never forgot this therapy: it was perhaps the greatest trauma of his life. A rubber bit was placed in his mouth, he was injected with tranquillisers, and an electric shock was delivered to his brain. 'It's like a horse kicking you in the head; you feel like an animal too,' he told Nurse Alice in his final days.

Eddie had few 'little luxuries', as he called them. He liked his John Player Blue and a few cans of beer if there was sport on television. Anyone could call to Eddie's pad—for money, to share a can, borrow a cigarette, discuss their troubles—and he would always let them in. He liked to set quizzes: 'Name six streets in Dublin named after counties in Ireland' was one he enjoyed best with new friends.

I thought of Eddie as a kind of psychiatrist, trained on the streets and the hospitals he was marched into. He spoke knowledgeably about people's problems and could do wonderful imitations of the many doctors who treated him over the years. I'm sure he did me too. He tolerated my dull company and occasional home visits probably because I would share a few of his cigarettes with him.

Eddie knew he had a mental illness, and he knew where it came from. 'It's inherited, and there's nothing I can do about it only accept it,' he would say. His problem was not his illness, it was how others treated him because of it.

In his one-room flat on the upper floor of a complex off Francis Street lived Eddie, his three Jack Russells, his Crombie coat, his television, a bed, a chair and his hob cooker, which doubled as a heater in winter.

He carried a photograph of himself looking very dapper as a young footballer. 'I've lived a weird life, like a hermit, lost for company—the stigma of mental illness lasts. Look at the new hospitals: you have to go in a separate entrance if you're mentally ill.'

Eddie had a twinkle in his eye and always found the right words in the company of ladies. He was considered a 'great catch' in his youth. He had the gift of the gab, liked his clothes, and knew just the right words to make others feel comfortable with him.

Like James, he would challenge those who assumed authority as their mantle. He noticed little things. Being a former boxer, he liked to keep people on their toes. During his final illness he would query why nobody seemed to have time to sit down and chat: 'the way they say how are your bowels today instead of how are you.'

When Eddie's time was up the hospice rang TRUST to say they were having difficulty getting him attached to a pain-killer pump. His fear of injections was very real: it reminded him of the sometimes brutal ways his mental illness was treated. Nurse Geraldine rushed off to Harold's Cross to comfort him. She held out her hand and he squeezed it. Gerri asked him to close his eyes. His last words were so typical of Eddie: he said, 'Thank you.'

Two wise men have left us this year at TRUST. We cherish their gift of wisdom and thank their families and friends for sharing them with us. (Oh, and Eddie's six counties that have Dublin streets named after them are Clare, Wicklow, Meath, Wexford, Cork and Kildare. The last one, Eddie would giggle, has the real madhouse in it!)

Maurice Guéret is a family doctor and a friend, board member and trustee of TRUST. He writes irreverent columns and illegible prescriptions, in equal measure.

In honour of Miss Beatrice Ryan

Jacqueline Hayden

I am the product of Donagh O'Malley's visionary decision to provide free education at the secondary level. As a result I was the first member of my family to get the chance to go to university. The social impact of Mr O'Malley's decision is well documented. Arguably the most important step on the road to the creation of equality of opportunity for all in education in Ireland (sadly, still a long way from being achieved), O'Malley's surprise announcement dramatically widened the horizons for many of the less well-off children of the 1950s.

Without being melodramatic, my horizons were literally 'changed utterly.' In September 1969 I took the number 70 bus out of Mulhuddart and started first year in Dominican College, Eccles Street. Donagh O'Malley gave me the start, but it was the many wonderful women teachers who 'wasted time with people,' including me, that allowed me to take full advantage of his initiative.

When I reflect on the essential elements of the education I received in Eccles Street I am always struck by one thing above all else: I was given time! I did not just study English or history with this or that teacher. I did not just receive a package of instruction that fulfilled a particular curriculum requirement. I was assisted on a path of discovery by teachers who did not see their role as confined by the school gate or the clock. I have so many memories of conversations, ideas being scattered in the ether, outings to theatres and galleries, as well as phenomenal encouragement and gestures of kindness that it is hard to pick out examples that would unearth for the reader the profound impact these women had on my development as a person.

One woman in particular stands out. Miss Beatrice Ryan taught me English and made me passionate about thinking. I knew Miss Ryan was an intellectual from the minute I sat in her class. I might have had a most unformed notion of what an intellectual was, but I knew she was one. Miss Ryan exuded an excitement about literature, language, ideas, music and thinking that made discovery and learning a joy. All my life I have not forgotten the first time Miss Ryan quoted Pascal: 'Man is but a reed, the weakest in nature, but he is a thinking reed.' I thought and thought about what this meant until my head hurt.

I think I was about fourteen when Miss Ryan handed me a book on the concept of pluralism, which included a contribution from Marshall McLuhan, the educator and philosopher famous, among other achievements, for his concept of the 'global village' and for coining the expression 'The medium is the message.' I was in a Catholic school run by Dominican nuns who employed a woman who was exploring the implications of the pluralist notion of the state at the start of what we now know to be a period of profound social change in Ireland. Miss Ryan was remarkable, but so were the Dominican sisters who ran Eccles Street.

At a time when any sensible adult is concerned about how alcohol is abused in Irish society and in particular by binge-drinking among the young, I have to be careful not to be understood to be extolling the virtues of drinking, but Miss Ryan graciously gave me my first glass of wine. More than thirty years later I can still remember the excitement of Miss Ryan's invitation to come to lunch at her home in Ballsbridge. It was a terrifically sunny Saturday as I and my friend Mary climbed the steps to the house Miss Ryan shared with members of her family, including her sister Florence, the pianist.

Sitting in Miss Ryan's sitting-room with its book-lined walls was the embodiment of Virginia Woolf's 'A room of one's own'. Miss Ryan never had to labour the idea of a woman's right to her own creative space. She did not have to labour a feminist message. It was implicit in her sensibilities. That day Mary and I had the privilege of being invited to her private space, and when she offered us a small glass of wine with our lunch (she did not drink at the time) I remember it as the moment when I knew I was on the brink of womanhood. Miss Ryan gave us more than lunch and a glass of wine that Saturday: she gave me a vision of a life; she gave me a sense of her sensibilities. Looked at from the viewpoint of some fashionable paradigms, Miss

Ryan had wasted a lot of her precious time that day; in fact it could be argued that all she gave over and above what was required involved her in wasting time with people. I think not.

The reader may well have already guessed my main point, that is, the macro-implications of my individual story of immense gratitude to an ethos in education personified in Beatrice Ryan and in many of the teachers and nuns who cared for me in Eccles Street. I do not intend to make a nostalgic point about the good old days. I am more concerned to use my experience as a warning that while fundamental change is required throughout the educational system, from primary to university level, the core element of learning and growth is in the relationship between teacher and student. My experience as a university lecturer over the last ten years leaves me very concerned that some of the structural and management changes at third level do not preserve or promote the interests of students. In fact the very welcome emphasis on excellence in research has not been mirrored, in some instances, by a similar concern to promote excellence in teaching standards and pastoral care among lecturers.

A range of factors and developments have indirectly led to the sidelining of teaching in some universities. It is now regarded as a cliché to talk about the impact of education on the making of the 'Celtic Tiger'. Enthusiastic talk of the positive role of a well-educated, intellectually rounded young population has now been dampened by concerns about the long-term economic impact of the dearth of mathematical and scientific qualifications among school-leavers. While educators may differ as to the scale or significance of this alleged poor interest and performance in maths and science subjects, there is no doubt that the response to the perceived problem from both Government and university heads has been to seek to give priority to science, maths and technological research at third level. Nothing wrong with this, merely the rectification of what had previously been a skewed conception of the role of education! Radical change was undoubtedly required to deal with policy, vision, practices and organisation at third-level institutions which, it is argued, retard 'cutting-edge' research and discourage top-class international scholars from accepting posts in academic institutions in Ireland.

So, as universities scramble to get higher up the league tables, resources are squeezed towards departments and disciplines whose lecturers produce internationally publishable research. Money is pinched from teaching budgets to support higher salaries to catch researchers who will advance the profile of the department and the university.

The fundamental issue at stake behind the so-called modernisation of Irish universities is not tradition and ethos versus the need for commercial management and functioning institutional systems but the fact that universities serve two masters. Universities are not institutions of advanced research alone: they also exist to pass on that learning and to nurture and shape the minds and characters of the student body. I am not alone in my concern about the disregard for undergraduate students and the low value put on teaching ability in the evaluation of potential lecturers. However, the public is generally not much interested in the goings-on in academia, so most will have missed the spats over academic poaching, rows over whether it's the university or the researcher that 'owns' research funding, not to forget the discreet flow of letters to editors from academics claiming that restructuring in this or that university is paying scant regard to the needs and interests of students. No thinking person opposes change for the sake of it, so expressing caution about the negative impact on the quality of teaching and the nature of the relationship between undergraduates and lecturers should not put one into the category of a Luddite.

In embracing business models and university league tables and giving priority to postgraduate research programmes, academic leaders should not forget that the capacity to inspire a thirst for knowledge and understanding is at the heart of what a university is about. Human interaction, time spent talking and listening is what promotes and helps satisfy that thirst. Placing a high value on teaching is not 'wasting time with people'; it is a rational investment in the nation's young, regardless of what paradigm or business model is informing academic decision-making.

Jacqueline Hayden was formerly an RTE journalist and current affairs producer. She is now a lecturer in the Department of Political Science, Trinity College, Dublin. Her most recent book is *The Collapse of Communist Power in Poland* (2006).

Time and destiny

Priscilla Jana

As an African woman, I grew up in South Africa under the terror of apartheid. During this time I witnessed and experienced some of the worst atrocities and crimes against humanity inflicted on people by people.

This is the heritage of millions of South Africans. It is a heritage we cannot change. Time spent can never be redeemed. Time wasted is life wasted.

Life is a stream flowing only in one direction. As the beautiful spring goes by, we know that it will be back again. The changing phases of the moon will come and go. When the sun sets it will certainly surge again; but the water that once flowed in the stream will never come back.

According to Heraclitus in 500 BC, 'Everything flows and nothing abides, everything gives way and nothing stays fixed. You cannot step twice in the same river, for other waters and yet others go flowing on.'

In 1994 the demise of apartheid ushered in a new dawn in South Africa. Yesterday was another country. Nelson Mandela, our first democratically elected president, guided the nation: 'And so we must, constrained by and yet regardless of the accumulated effect of our historical burdens, seize the time to define for ourselves what we want to make of our shared destiny.'

We South Africans became acutely aware of time and destiny. We had to control time as an evolutionary force to effect the change we dreamed of. So, we chose to focus on the future rather than the past, on understanding rather than vengeance, on reparation rather than retaliation, and on *ubuntu* rather than victimisation.

As Africans we are blessed with the philosophy of *ubuntu*. *Ubuntu* is the philosophy of humanity. Expressed in Sotho, '*Motho ka motho ba batho babang,*' it means that 'human beings are human beings because of other human beings.'

Fundamental to *ubuntu* is the uncompromised conviction that human life has equal worth. '*Motho ka motho ka ana boshlana*': 'Human beings are human beings, and there are no lesser human beings.'

Ubuntu embraces truth, equality, fairness, political freedom, respect for human dignity and a just social order.

The spiritual foundation of *ubuntu* is embedded in human solidarity. *Ubuntu* connects all humanity in a universal bond, cemented by compassion, sharing and caring. This affinity of *ubuntu* leads to the profound sense of being united with the richness of diversity. W. B. Yeats spells out this purpose in 'The Coming of Wisdom with Time':

> Though leaves are many, the root is one;
> Through all the lying days of my youth
> I swayed my leaves and flowers in the sun;
> Now I may wither into the truth.

If human and intellectual potential are our most important resources, then *ubuntu* is our most creative response.

Ubuntu involves the understanding that the dignity of any one person is inextricably linked to the dignity of other persons. The degradation, the exploitation, the suffering of any human being must therefore affect us all. This ethic is expounded by John Donne:

> No man is an island, entire of itself . . . Any man's death diminishes me, because I am involved in mankind; and therefore never send to know for whom the bell tolls; it tolls for thee.

The truth is that we live in an unequal world. As certain nations are advancing exponentially with economic globalisation and technological explosion, the reality is that millions of people around the world are yet denied life's chances and continue to live in gross indignity.

Has today's high-tech age of instant gratification and consumerism corroded our principles, our values, our attitudes? Have we forgotten how to give, how to care for others? Have we lost our ability to nurture? More poignantly, do we permit the penetrating pace of life to simply swallow up precious time?

The poet Rabindranath Tagore analogises how 'the butterfly counts not months but moments, and has time enough.'

The profound effect of time is not how much we can get out of life but how much we can give to others to make this world a better place for all. Every human being has something that is equal, that is, time.

Many ancient philosophers, scientists and poets have written incisively about time. One of the earliest recorded philosophies of time was expounded by the philosopher and vizier Ptahhtep in the 24th century BC. 'Do not lessen the time of following desire, for the wasting of time is an abomination to the spirit.'

We need to take time to care and to practise in our hearts the real essence of *ubuntu*, that 'I am because you are.' *Ubuntu* is grounded in respect and understanding for all human beings. As we learn to respect and understand each other we promote the interconnectedness where we learn to give time as part of a natural order. This true giving can make a difference to life. Fundamental human rights can be ensured and dignity and respect can be restored to all humankind.

As globalisation trails an interdependence among nations, *ubuntu* traces our collective moral and historical obligations to all the peoples of the world.

Ultimately, there must be a greater fulfilment in the philosophy of *ubuntu* than in an aggressively, individualistic, competitive and selfish way of life. This philosophy of time and destiny is appropriated by Shakespeare in *Macbeth*:

Tomorrow, and tomorrow, and tomorrow
Creeps in this petty pace from day to day
To the last syllable of recorded time,
And all our yesterdays have lighted fools
The way to dusty death.

Priscilla Jana is the ambassador of South Africa to Ireland. She has devoted her career as a lawyer almost entirely to the field of civil liberties and human rights. She was a human rights lawyer in a majority of the celebrated political trials in South Africa. Before taking up her appointment in Ireland she served as ambassador of South Africa in the Netherlands.

All hands on deck

Rachel Joynt

What happened? When did it all start to change? These questions are on the tip of my tongue when I listen to my parents and hear the stories of the front door of the house always being left open or indeed the key left in the door at all times when they were growing up—all this so that neighbours and friends could come and go as they pleased. Everyone in the same area and street would know each other for years—raised each other's children, practically.

The biggest thing that stuck in my mind was that everyone would look out for each other. If a neighbour or friend was sick it would be 'all hands on deck.' The dinner would be prepared and the children looked after as well as looking after their own. There was always time for charitable work, either by calling in to an elderly neighbour for a chat and a cup of tea or collecting toys for a local children's charity. Efforts were endless to help those less fortunate than yourself. Time was spent chatting and listening to each other, caring about what was going on in each other's lives. Even though work had to be carried out during the day, there was always time for people, either to chat or if help was needed.

All this sounds unbelievable today. The thought of the front door being left open, or the key left in the lock throughout the day, I find quite frightening. Our society has changed dramatically from the time when my parents were growing up, with a lot more disposable cash floating about. We have all become more materialistic. We all have many more expensive possessions and so feel the need to lock them away, safe and out of harm's way. These items give us status and in our minds some sort of meaning. We fear those who probably cannot afford them.

This is one reason many of us are afraid to waste time with people. We have become caught up in having the best of everything, which is not necessarily a bad thing, but we are tending to divide our society through our obsession with material things.

As most of us are now commuting to and from work, working long hours to pay for our materialistic life-style, we have little time for anything else. When we get a chance to relax it's more than likely it is in front of our new 50-inch flat-screen television, bought out of last month's pay packet.

Where did our new materialist attitudes come from? When did the idea of sharing become something we turn our noses up at? When did we become indifferent about those less fortunate who are being left behind?

If people do not conform to what is considered normal in our society they are shunned, and become outsiders. They are left out and consigned to a lonely life, with little or no real human contact. It is said that money can't buy you happiness. However, there is no doubt it can ease burdens and help you live a very comfortable life; but what is it all worth without love and respect?

I am still trying to understand why we do not even know who lives next door. When walking down the street I often find myself wondering, when I see a homeless person, Where will he or she sleep tonight? I watch people walking past the homeless person and I wonder, Can they actually see that person in the doorway? But that's the thing, though: they do see, yet they choose to ignore and walk straight by and carry on shopping. Busy, busy, busy, and no time to stop and do something out of this world, like ask that person in the doorway if they are all right, or go to a shop and hand them some food, as they have probably not eaten in hours, or even since the day before.

The only thing we can probably observe with certainty is that we have become very wrapped up in ourselves. No-one seems to 'make' time to involve themselves with other people from any walk of life any more. We all seem totally focused on 'getting ahead,' but instead of 'getting ahead' are we falling far behind? One day will we all be too busy to even talk to each other? Could we become vulnerable? What happens if we cannot keep up and find ourselves excluded? Is it possible that we might crave the friendly smile, the pat on the hand, and to be told, 'Everything is going to be just fine,' except there will be no-one left to care?

We should all waste time with others, because one day we may need someone to waste time with us.

Rachel Joynt, a native of Galway, is a student garda based in the Dublin South-Central Division. In 2005 she received a bachelor of business studies (honours) degree in hotel and catering management.

The lost art of arsing

Eamon Keane

Time . . . you only think of it when it is too late. I remember spending a lot of time with my father, Eamon. I never got to see him before he died. It troubled me greatly for a time.

A few years after his death I got to know a wonderful jazz player called Chris St Ledger. I was wasting time when a friend said I should go and visit Chris when he was very ill. So I was with him before he died. Recently in Malawi I was with a woman in the hours before she died of AIDS. Those times sort of squared it up in terms of my dad. God bless time-wasting.

When my uncle John B. Keane was very ill I had learnt by that stage the importance of wasting time. I was working for RTE but I took time off and went down to Listowel, where his wonderful family were nursing him around the clock. On the following weekend he told myself and my cousin John to go to Cardiff for the Munster rugby match. But how could we when he was very ill? John B. insisted, as he knew the importance of wasting time at a rugby match when things were tough.

I learnt the importance of wasting time when as a kid I stayed with my grandmother in Ardmore, Co. Waterford; days on the Curragh beach just playing and being. I lost that art over the years. I rediscovered it when I left college. I had time on my hands and got involved in voluntary work—what a brilliant waste of time! I learnt about myself and my own wounds through working with others. I had fun and fear in equal measure.

My Aunt Sheila in Cahersiveen has a great expression—*arsing*. 'What are you doing, Sheila?'—'Arsing.'

Arsing is a lost art. People will pay hundreds of euros for weekends away to 'discover your inner piglet.' You don't need to. Start arsing more regularly. Get up out of the bed or whatever article of comportment you are reading this in. Walk down the road and don't be afraid to say hello to someone, even a car-clamper. If you can, stop at some point and look upwards and notice the things you never noticed before. Yeah, like the sky.

It's all about ecology. We need time-wasters. We have too many busy people, and the environment is suffering. Look at the gobdaw who walks for ten minutes with the mobile phone attached to his ear, shouting at the top of his voice. Whose benefit is this show of plumage for?

Contrast him with the fella I meet each morning on the way in to work at Newstalk. I walk up the Grand Canal and there is a guy on the bench each morning. 'John' has his few cans, whatever newspaper he has managed to find, and an oul' sandwich. Bum, some might call him. John is not, though. John makes me pause when he looks at me. John makes me think how lucky I am that I didn't fall by the way of alcoholism or the underlying emotional distress that rips people apart.

I am usually worrying about some interview with some politician when I pass John. However, John makes me remember why it is important to look for truth. A bit poncy? No. Sometimes you tend to think that everyone who is not part of your world doesn't count. You will not hear John interviewed for focus groups or mortgage discussions. (By the way, why is there never a property programme discussion on homelessness?)

How much time do you waste in front of the television, our new altar of reflection? I knew things were bad when the other night I found myself watching rat wrestling from Bangkok on Eurosport. I could have been wasting time talking to a family or friend, or someone who needed a call or a visit.

We live in gated communities to keep people out. We drive in big jeeps to assert our place in the hierarchical structure, dark windows to keep the lesser ones from looking in. We are afraid to go out with our normal skin: it needs to be augmented in some way. We don't waste time, for fear of contamination.

When I was in Malawi with the Rose Project half of me was scared to Jesus that I would pick up an infection or a bug from the 'poor starving HIV-infected orphans.' Then the child smiles at you and you relax and forget all your prejudices. You come home and think about how you avoid certain people—people who are difficult to listen to, who unnerve you or even annoy you.

I'll go back to my dad. I used to feel that time I spent with him was a waste of time, because he could not see my things my way. But time spent is never wasted. It is how we show, however inarticulately, that we love someone, and ultimately that time is the peace we can harvest when that someone is gone. So go get wasting that time . . .

Eamon Keane is a native of Co. Kerry. He comes from a family with strong media connections: son of the actor Eamon, nephew of the Kerry legend John B. Keane, and brother of the BBC reporter Fergal Keane. He presents 'Lunchtime' on Newstalk daily and has also worked for the BBC and South African Broadcasting Corporation. He has directed and presented three television documentaries for RTE, including the acclaimed 'Fields of Gold' on the Munster rugby great Mick Galwey. A sports enthusiast, Eamon religiously follows the Munster rugby team around Europe. His other love is music, and he has performed at sold-out gigs in such venues as the Sugar Club in Dublin. Eamon does not live with a wife and three children in Wicklow, nor does he love collecting butterflies.

The little village

Michael 'Babs' Keating

Nobody arrives at Croke Park by accident. You have the exceptional ones who have started out at juvenile level and made it out of the thousands; but it's the commitment of all the people at those levels that puts the players on the field. What the GAA is meant to do is to unite parishes and keep people together.

I was lucky enough to grow up in a hurling environment. My father and the village of Grange were huge Tipperary hurling supporters. In the 40s you might have a radio in one house, and then when rural electrification came in the 50s you had the voice of all the matches relayed into every house. In '49, '50 and '51 a young bunch of hurlers emerged, and they went on to win three all-Irelands. We put pictures of them on our walls. They were our heroes. I remember a teacher going around, asking what we wanted to be when we grew up. Two guys wanted to be priests (and they are), and I wanted to be a hurler. But I suppose I forgot that hurling was not a professional sport, so I had to be something else as well.

In the late 50s and early 60s tractor power came to farms, and in my place near Clonmel we were in the Golden Vale, prosperous countryside. Esso employed all-Ireland medal-holders as salesmen. I had played in three minor all-Ireland finals by then. At the age of eighteen I joined Esso and went on the road, selling.

I suppose the GAA has been my life. My whole life has been dedicated to it. Luckily my wife came from the same place, and she understood. I made mistakes but I was never dishonest, and I was never afraid to advise young men who I had responsibility for.

I was the Tipperary manager when we won the all-Ireland in 1989 after a seventeen-year gap. Because of that it brought new pressure on players. On the way home we arranged a meeting so we could plan our future. We stopped in the Montague Hotel in Port Laoise, and I told them I was going to say the most important words they would hear in their careers. I saw the future for them, and I saw the future pitfalls. I warned them that there were players who won all-Irelands and then their own families, wives and friends weren't good enough for them. There are some people out there who would be better people if they had lost in Croke Park instead of winning.

I had heard so many stories and seen so many players who ruined their lives. It starts in the public house with excessive drinking: like most situations in life, drink has been really the start.

There is a lesson that wider society can learn from sport. For me to have my name on a Croke Park programme, coming from a small place like Grange, meant that everybody would have had an involvement. I was aware of the need to give due respect and due thanks to those people. There is the pride of the little village, and they share my glory. Today's culture of selfishness and consumerism takes somewhat from that selflessness.

When we set up the Tipperary Supporters' Club in the 1980s there was high unemployment and inflation. I did not know how many of my potential players would be there to play, whether they might be working in Boston or walking the streets of Sydney. So the Supporters' Club played a huge role in raising funds for the team.

I took on the managership of the team again recently, and it was important for me as I fade into the mist and wilderness of this game that I tried my very best to put these young players on the right road.

I had a lot of disappointments and hurt within the GAA. The biggest thing that has changed the scene is the opportunity for everybody out there to express an opinion, from local radio to the press, and to use that voice without knowing the background. We can all be experts without playing the game.

When I first entered the Tipperary dressing-room I told them I needed a huge commitment and that everybody had to understand there could be no pretenders. Individualism was out the door, and there should be no singling out individuals as heroes. It's not an individual sport, it's a team effort, and any reward should be offered to the whole team. It's a contradiction to create individuals.

After we lost to Wexford I got phone calls at 2 a.m., text messages and abuse from people I thought were friends. I just do not want to know that side of the GAA.

I think the GAA has a huge exercise ahead of itself to maintain the standards and maintain the hurling. It is one of the best games in the world. But football is easy to organise. It's not easy to organise young lads with hurleys and helmets. They are expensive, and the time has come for the GAA to stop investment in bricks and mortar and start investing in people.

My friends today would be the guys I started off playing with at juvenile level. You do not think about that when you are young and starting out. Those days pressures were different. I was married at twenty-four, which was very early by today's standards. I had a mortgage, a home and a young family. Frank Purcell was a year ahead of me at school. We backed horses together in those early years. He cycled to school from five miles one side of the village and I cycled from seven miles the other side, and we played on the football team. During our lunch hour the country lads had our own canteen, or we could go down town and chat up girls from the Presentation.

I came to Dublin thirty years ago, and when I started the Tipperary Supporters' Club he was a big part of it. He had a hard time, and there were nights when we walked the park together. Then, just when everything had turned right financially and at home, he had the heart attack. His death has been a huge loss to me.

Michael 'Babs' Keating is a dual Tipperary GAA player. He managed the Tipperary senior hurling team from late 1986 to 1994 and again from late 2005 to 2007, winning all-Irelands in 1989 and 1991. As a player he won three all-Ireland senior hurling medals (1964, 1965 and 1971) and numerous other hurling and football medals for club, county, and Munster. He also won an All-Star and a Texaco Hurler of the Year Award (1971). In 1986 he founded the Tipperary Supporters' Club, the first GAA supporters' club, which continues to thrive.

Balloons to you

Paddy Kelly

Homelessness
Love your home,
no matter how humble, how small
there are many, many,
who have no home at all.

Love your home,
be grateful, be aware,
your kindness will ease and hearten others,
let them know you care.

Balloons to You
My friends in TRUST
take a balloon
upon that balloon
write all your dreams
then set it free and follow it.

Paddy Kelly is a long-time friend of TRUST, now residing in St John's Nursing
Home.

No losers: Talking beats television

Colum Kenny

An American way of using the word 'loser' has gradually wormed its way into common parlance in Ireland in recent years. When children call someone a 'loser' they jeer as much as speak the term, and it is intended to be hurtful. A 'loser' in this sense is someone who is weak or awkward (although not obviously disabled) or someone who fails to conform to the social expectations of their peers. It is a vile usage.

As people once thought that by just looking into the eyes of a person dying of famine they could condemn themselves to a similar death, so people shy away from contact with 'losers'. 'Losers' drag us down. And we do not like to be reminded how close to the edge of the precipice we all stand.

The word 'loser' has been adopted here off American television shows. Cheap and superficially cheerful, American pap bulks out the schedules of many television channels and is consumed in large quantities, especially by younger viewers. Those who do not swim in this audiovisual sea are likely to sound unknowing among their peers, and so risk being considered 'losers'. If you have no mobile phone, are not using Bebo or some similar web site, have no e-mail address and cannot discuss last night's television, then where are you?

Television influences the way in which people see the world, not least by setting agendas or framing issues. If the vast majority of those whom we see on television are never portrayed as taking time to read a book, or pray, or meditate, or engage in random or regular acts of compassion and charity, then the likelihood of our regarding such behaviour as worth while, normative or necessary is lessened.

Media also influence our behaviour by filling up time, by capturing our heads. When there is so much to distract or entertain us (and much of it, far from mere pap, quite clever), then it is easy to sink into the passive and receptive mode where time is passed rather than appreciated. We enjoy the stimulation, which relieves boredom and allows us to escape our worries. We prefer wasting time with the telly to spending time with awkward or demanding people.

We live longer than earlier generations. The official working week is shorter. We have more holidays and lots of fine inventions to wash dishes or clean clothes or get places faster than our ancestors ever thought possible. We spend lots of time, perhaps too much, around our spouses and children. We also socialise with our friends, particularly in pubs or restaurants. A remarkable number of fine eating establishments are busy much of the time in modern Ireland. It was not always so.

And there is plenty of money around to pay for fine meals, compared with earlier decades. People have things to do, places to go. They are not hanging about waiting for something to happen. Expensive tickets for concerts, theatrical events and games are snapped up months in advance. We are busy having a good time. Turkey or Tenerife this year, darling? Both, of course.

And we are busy being busy, earning money to support our varied life-styles while coping with the indicators of economic expansion, such as long commutes and clogged roads and overtime and child care. The sofa seems so welcoming at the end of a tiring day, and the remote so easy to flick.

We feel under pressure. Money cares recur despite the boom; and our children face threatening complexities; and job security is evaporating; and health care is problematic. Don't tell me your troubles: I've got troubles of my own. So why spend time seeking out other contacts, spending time with people who will just bring us down? Don't we pay social workers and the like to take care of that kind of thing?

A cynic might say that people once spent more time with one another because they had far less to do. I mean, before television, what *was* there to do? For our part we fill our leisure time with leisure activities. One suspects that the capacity to dodge the burden of other people's lives expands to fill the time available.

People require a reason to listen to others who are of no direct benefit or interest to them. It is easy to listen to those whom we fancy and desire, or those whose family or commercial fortunes are entwined with ours. Taste and self-interest motivate us to hear them out, at least at some surface level. Even here we may not really be listening to the person, just appearing to do so in order to be polite.

And why should we listen any deeper? Why should we listen at all to those with whom we have no immediate connection? Some people articulate religious arguments for compassion, others secular ones: both can be quite self-interested in different ways. The religious person who acts compassionately in order to get a spiritual reward in the next life seems to me to be no more virtuous than a person who listens to someone because they get paid to do so. And the secular argument that society is a sort of social contract (where we ought to treat others well because we may need them to treat us well) is purely pragmatic. There is a related religious argument that our true happiness depends on the happiness of others. Nevertheless, it is the case that such motivations at least result in actions that are more beneficial to those in need than is our ignoring or spurning people who want someone to listen.

So is there any reason to spend time with people that is not ultimately self-interested in some way? Can anyone honestly believe that it is simply 'the right thing to do'? There have been instances when it seemed that people acted entirely selflessly, but they are rare. But there are degrees of selfishness, and spending time with people in need is not something that *has* to be selfless. What matters is that people understand that there is a range of reasons why it is a good idea for them to do so. People can be taught these things at school: they are not taught them always.

Religions also have a role in educating people to happiness at a more complex level than that of material satisfaction. In the modern world religion has been discredited in many respects, because of the excesses and narrowness of too many Christian and Muslim leaders: people may never see the beautiful side of the wisdom traditions, or encounter practitioners to whom truth is an experience rather than a dogma.

Politicians too can play a role, outlining visions of society that are broad and inspirational. Today, many politicians barely question the prevalent and unsustainable market ideology: they pay only lip service to other dimensions of reality. When productivity is elevated like an idol then it is not surprising that even in the sphere of public services one finds managerial impatience with staff members who 'waste time' on people with problems.

The media too have a role to play in opening people's eyes to what lies beyond the immediate. With the diminution of public-service broadcasting ideals, television has become even more dependent on advertising and on a culture of consumerism that feels threatened by the notion of idle time or 'listening'. But the media have moral responsibilities as well as commercial imperatives.

On an individual basis, it actually feels good to talk and listen outside the ordinary or everyday requirements of our lives: to lose the baggage. It can also be a bit threatening, reducing the space for our own ego (unless we are merely 'listening' in a largely patronising way), and may give rise to feelings of long-term obligation or duty. It is hard to stop surfing and just be patient.

Perhaps that is why people like me tell ourselves that we discharge our responsibilities to those in need by writing about them, by listening in the abstract and by articulating their needs through articles and lectures. The fact that such articles and lectures are what we do anyway is very handy, killing two birds with the one stone, as it were.

I believe that we should try consciously to make time to listen to people, to those near us whom we may take for granted and to those more distant from us whom we can still help. I have been convinced that it is the right thing to do, and that it is advisable if we hope to be happy.

But I do not do it nearly enough, even in the case of my immediate family. When I occasionally try to do it I become self-conscious and have an irritating tendency to seem condescending. So I am grateful for the invitation to contribute to this book, because it has forced me to reflect on my own failings in that respect.

Colum Kenny is associate professor of communications at Dublin City University and a regular columnist in the *Sunday Independent*. His books include *Moments that Changed Us: Ireland, 1973–2005* (2005) and a collection of poetry entitled *Standing on Bray Head* (1995).

Random thoughts

Mary Kotsonouris

It is not difficult to observe that some of our friends are clearly wasting their time, spending it with all kinds of odd people, quite often with lonely individuals who want to tell some rambling story or recite boring reminiscences heard far too often—people who are unattractive and self-centred; nobody likes them. Plainly we can so easily find an excuse to avoid such visits. 'Anyway,' we tell our friends, 'they don't appreciate it.'

What do we mean? There are parallel interpretations of the word 'appreciate': one is to be grateful for an act of kindness and another is to understand and acknowledge the effort of work that has to be put into that act. For example, to make a cake someone got the ingredients together, might even have had to go out to buy them, stood around a hot oven, and worried a bit that it might not be successful. Perhaps their effort deserves some slight pause for thought rather than 'Oh, thanks. You really shouldn't have bothered,' rather than reflecting on the impulse that made the giver want to give pleasure to someone. Perhaps there is not even a gruff word of thanks for your foolish friend. The recipient may feel, logically enough, that he or she never asked for the cake, the visit, the time, whatever. Or then again, perhaps that is not what it is about at all.

There are others who have no option with their time except to waste it. Little wonder that in former days visiting prisoners was considered to be a corporal work of mercy. It cannot be easy regularly going through the security procedures, sitting around in cold, ugly places, most of all trying to think of things to say to someone who may have lost all notion of what life is like outside his barred and circumscribed daily existence. Prisoners, especially those serving a life sentence, are frequently depressed, lacklustre and relentlessly sorry for themselves; they rarely seem to make friends with other inmates. Yet families are remarkably loyal to them—respectable, harmless people on whom the son or brother has brought shame and yet they face into all that maybe every Sunday, burdened with love, albeit exasperated love, loyalty, pity and perhaps even guilt, however unmerited, because they are free, have a family, a home and a job.

Every place, if you look, you can see people wasting their time: standing on a wet street with a collection box for the poor, the missions, the hospice, abandoned dogs, or trudging out on a winter's night with the Vincent de Paul; you might even notice them on that seemingly most hopeless of pastimes, gathering together to demand common humanity for far-away Burma.

On a summer's day in the middle of an unlikely heat wave I was crossing Capel Street Bridge during lunch hour. At the corner of Essex Street and the quays a couple of elderly tourists had waylaid an executive type dressed smartly in his summer gear and forced to jam his leather briefcase between his feet to look at the street map they had handed to him. I thought with idle malice how he must have been badly caught in the buffeting stream of people. The lady was pointing to some particular spot on the map, and as I passed them I heard the young man say, 'Yes, I know, but I'm trying to see if I can find you a nicer way to get there.'

Mary Kotsonouris is a writer and a former judge of the District Court.

The conversation

Mick Lacey

Sitting outside the Royal Spa Hotel in Lisdoonvarna sipping coffee, enjoying late afternoon sunshine recently talking to Skippy about the benefits of the mobile phone, how you could instantly dial up and speak to a person in any part of the world: in Timbuktu, the USA or even Australia. Skippy is going there next month for his sixtieth birthday, and he had just finished a conversation with his brother Jimmy, who emigrated to Australia on an assisted passage in 1965 for ten pounds, when he was seventeen years of age. Skippy emigrated from Dublin to Lisdoonvarna thirty years ago, on a rough passage via the Fleadh Cheoil in Ennis in 1977.

Skippy's real name is Anthony Oliver Reid. He was born in Crampton Buildings in the centre of Dublin in 1947 and was Mickser Reid's first cousin. Crampton Buildings were at one time local authority flats, now much sought-after apartment dwellings, off Temple Bar. Skippy lived there with his five sisters and two brothers, and if you applied for a job or had a date with a mott you would change your address to Bedford Row, an adjacent street, better-sounding and with no history.

At one time in Dublin everybody knew Mickser Reid. Rather than being hampered in any way by his short stature, on the contrary he put his size and wit to gigantic use. Mickser featured in all the well-known pantomimes in Dublin of the 50s and early 60s in the Theatre Royal and the Gaiety. I remember him being blown out of a gas cooker in one of the pantos, which starred such famous artistes and comedians as Maureen Potter, Danny Cummins and Jimmy O'Dea.

On one occasion, Skippy explained, when Mickser was due to play in the panto matinée at the Gaiety he had a dreadful hangover after the opening the previous night. He was referred by Joey Betts, another well-known Dublin character, who was partial to a bottle of gin or two and well experienced in the art of managing hangovers, to the pharmacist. Louie the Fix was the pharmacist's nickname, famous for prescribing wonderful, rare, miraculous cures for all sorts of ailments.

Louie gave Mickser a magic concoction, assuring him that it would cure his head. During the afternoon's performance Mickser froze and couldn't move and had to be taken away in an ambulance, still standing erect like a statute. He had a type of seizure resembling rigor mortis. Louie had prescribed a chemical that had the effect of locking all his joints, leaving him stiff and rigid as a poker for the best part of the day.

Poor old Mickser ended up as a nipper or tea-boy on the building site of Hawkins House, following the demolition of the Theatre Royal and Regal Rooms, and later of the Metropole, the Capitol Cinema and the Prince's Bar, off O'Connell Street. (A nipper was the boy or man who made the tea on a building site and could be a person of any age.) The Capitol Cinema was built, on a smaller scale, like La Scala Opera House in Milan and was itself originally called La Scala. It was earthquake-proof, like its mother in Milan.

While discussing the benefits of the mobile phone we were joined by Peter Curtin, who owns the Roadside Tavern around the corner and was on his break. 'Oh, yes,' says Peter, 'God be with the days of the windy-upper, the oul' windy-upper phone. We had one in the pub up to a few years ago.'

'I remember,' said Skippy.

Peter explained that when you wanted to make a phone call you wound the handle gently, picked up the phone, and informed the local part-time telephonist who you wished to speak to. If it was a local call she then connected you to that person. There was only one telephone line in the town, and the ten or twelve phones in the town were all interconnected. If the operator wanted to call the priest's house that was one ring, the doctor's house two rings, the pub three rings, etc. If you possessed a phone, which few people in the town did at that time, you had to be very attentive and count the number of rings on the phone to identify who it was for. It was most difficult to make a unilateral phone call, as people were generally finding it confusing to know who was telephoning who.

While there were less people talking to each other on the phone then, there were certainly more people listening—oh, yes, listening. Perhaps that was where the concept of conferencing originated. Now, Peter said sadly, people don't listen any more; they just talk and talk.

'Yes,' said Skippy, 'and one day when a German wanted to make a phone call and asked how many times you wound the handle, we told him once for every mile. If he was ringing Dublin he had to wind it two hundred times non-stop, and if he was contacting Germany, well, sin scéal eile.'

'Ah, no, really what happened,' Peter interrupted, 'the German wanted to phone home, so I demonstrated to him how he should go about it. He was at that for a good ten minutes or so, with no response. Eventually he got somewhat impatient and commenced winding the handle rapidly and for longer periods. When the handle was wound it sent a signal that set a bell ringing in the telephonist's house. The dust must have been scattering and pictures falling off the wall with the ringing and piercing noise of the bell. Eventually she answered. The German told her he wanted to make a call to Germany to his girl-friend. "Put down the phone, have £4 in single shillings ready, and I'll call you back," the operator responded politely.

'The telephonist had to call Ennis, Ennis had to call Limerick, and Limerick had to call the exchange in Dublin, then Dublin would contact the exchange in Germany. They would then contact the exchange in his home town, and so on.

'Eventually when contact was made the telephonist rang the German in the pub. A large number of persons would be unwilling (or perhaps willing) listeners to these conversations at the time.

'The telephonist contacted the German. She told him to commence putting his money in the slot. It took him time to put the eighty single shillings into the phone; each shilling registered at the operator's end, so she would know exactly how much was being inserted. Just as the German heard the last shilling drop, 'Time up,' the telephonist interjected and politely pulled out the jack plug, disconnecting him. Some people said she got great pleasure doing this, having the house dust and cobwebs scattered all around her house as a result of the German's over-enthusiastic winding; others said rules are rules.

'Ah, people had loads of time then, they didn't rush. Even making a phone call was an occasion involving a lot of people, a community effort, so to speak,' Peter concluded, sighing.

'And before that we had smoke signals,' says Skippy.

'But you can't beat the mobile phone in an emergency, I suppose,' replied Peter.

Skippy added: 'Did you ever notice in Dublin everybody seems to be talking on their mobile phones?—bumping into each other, in cars and trucks; they don't see who's in front of them. People don't look at each other; you don't seem to know that many people in Dublin any more. The only people who look at you now, or make eye contact, are the street people, ones begging or busking or selling the *Big Issue*, maybe the odd copper or security man. People are very busy, have important things to do: spend their money, rushing, pushing, queuing, darting. I don't know anyone in Crampton Buildings or Temple Bar, and no-one knows me. A different breed of people lives there now. Dublin's like any big city now; it doesn't seem to stop.

'I remember,' says Skippy after a long pause, 'in Dublin not so long ago around six or half past a lull would come over the city. It seemed to slow down after the rush, with the traffic noise subsiding and the sun shining on a watery evening in late spring or autumn around St Stephen's Green, and you could hear the seagulls and people's footsteps. It was like suddenly a mystical quality would envelop the city and it was easy, and you'd never know who you would meet. Now it never appears to stop or slow down; 24-7, as they say. The young people seem to have a great time buzzing all over the place, with their New Age faces: not a pockmark, blackhead or pimple in sight. And beautiful straight teeth and noses, and polished heads, and their clothes on inside out showing off the labels, and self-cleaning runners; not like the ancient old crooked-nosed faces we have; and they seem to speak different. They look better, it's true, but some of them are awful fat. I found it a lonely city when I was up there recently at a funeral, not like before, or perhaps we're just getting older.'

'Do you recall,' I said, 'in the late 50s or early 60s, in a sort of run-down lodgings hotel in Talbot Street one of the residents, a middle-aged man, blasted the proprietor to death with a shotgun. His motive for killing him, he stated to investigating gardaí, was that he wanted the public to know that people lived there. That was evidence of a lonely city back then.'

'Is it better or worse now?' wondered Skippy. 'Well, there are murders every week now—shootings. People don't even mention them. Back then a murder was a ginormous topical issue. I love living here: the people of this town have always been great to me, they know your name and wave when they're passing in their cars, recognising and acknowledging your existence. Cities can become too indifferent. People don't seem to have any time for a chat, except on the mobile.'

'Oh, by the way, Skippy,' says I, 'speaking of time, when you get the time will you write out the words of that song about the fisherman who caught the crab and put it in the pisspot where the missus used to piss? You sang it at your party last week.'

'Only thing,' replied Skippy, 'only thing is that the last three people who asked me for the words of that song, by a strange coincidence when I gave it to them they died.'

'In that case, when it came to matters of life and death and the supernatural, and in the interests of self-preservation,' I said, 'forget about it.'

'Now it doesn't stop, the traffic and crowds are still rushing till God knows when,' added Skippy, 'and it's rough if you don't have money or plastic money or drink link cards; it's all plastic transactions now.'

'Speaking about money,' says Peter, eying Skippy, 'that reminds me, what about the fifty euros you owe me?'

'What fifty euros is that, Peter?' responded Skippy.

'The fifty you borrowed from me at Christmas,' replied Peter.

'No, Peter,' Skippy quietly contradicted him, 'you owe me fifty euros.'

'How do you make that out, Skippy?' says Peter.

'Well, remember at Christmas I asked you for a hundred euros and you only gave me fifty euros. Well, you still owe me the other fifty, so there you are,' responded Skippy brazenly.

'Yeah,' says Peter, 'I see why ya don't need any plastic cards around here. Well, some people don't anyway.'

'Does anyone remember when plastic came out first?' says Peter. 'Well, one time me and the brother saved a pound over a year and we went to Galway and bought these plastic soldiers ... By the way, before I continue, I was always wondering why do they call you Skippy,' he asked.

'Ah, well, that's a long story,' drawled Skippy. 'Have yous another five minutes?'

Michael Lacey was born in the Liberties of Dublin and now lives in Co. Clare. He qualified as an electrician with the ESB before entering Trinity College, Dublin, as a mature student. He is now a professionally qualified social worker in private practice and engages in training and teaching with the Health Service Executive, the National University of Ireland and the University of Limerick while also playing music in Co. Clare 'when they let me.'

It's the little things

Aine Lawlor

We use the word 'care' a lot these days. Care is what vulnerable people need: the old, the young, the sick. Care is what a caring society provides. But care takes time, the time of women largely, and now that more and more women are in paid employment, care comes from people who are often paid much less than the family members they are replacing.

So we want care, but we don't want to pay for it. On the other hand, paying for care, even at the lowly rates of pay carers can expect, is a huge burden on the families of the young, the disabled, the elderly. Care in the community is the first priority for most older people and those with disability, those with mental illness. It's a phrase that's tossed around a lot by politicians and health service chiefs. To be cared for in our own homes, to avoid 'being locked away,' no matter how nice the institution, is what we all want for ourselves if we are ever vulnerable and needy.

But. The 'but' is, to make care in the community work you need community members, family, neighbours, friends, who have the time to be there. And you need a joined-up health service that is able to join all the dots of the care plan, efficiently and flexibly. You need committed, professional staff, who stay in the job long enough to know their clients and have enough experience to be able to deal with their problems. These are the basic requirements of care in the community.

Six years ago my father suffered a series of minor strokes at the age of sixty-nine. An operation to clear the blocked artery that was the cause of those strokes resulted in a major stroke. After nine months in hospital he returned home on a 'care in the community' scheme. There was little enough my father could do after he recovered from his operation: he couldn't talk or walk or toilet himself. Trapped inside the wreck of his body, my father was as aware and as real as ever, raging at his incapacity. The only light at the end of the awful tunnel he faced was the chance to live again in his own home. Thanks to the commitment of his doctor, he got that chance. Despite all the ups and downs and occasional hardships he has endured since then, I don't think he has regretted going home for one minute.

So, as a family we have five years' experience of care in the community, with my father living in his home, relying on carers who come in several times a day to dress him, feed him, do the things for him he can't do for himself. Besides the carers there is a network of others, fantastic neighbours and friends, physiotherapists, occupational therapists, chiropodists, public health nurses, a committed GP—everything, it would seem, needed to make care in the community work.

Compared with many others in situations similar to ours, we have been incredibly lucky. Despite various problems, Daddy is able to rule the roost still in his own home, to live a life that in some way allows him to be the man he still is inside. The scheme that allows this is not available throughout the country. It goes without saying that it should be.

But. The 'but' is how he and his family have been hurt at times by the problems I outlined above. The time he needs and the time we don't have, all with children and jobs and only two in the same city as him. Discovering that behind every care plan is a bureaucracy that can frustrate and break even the most stout-hearted. The frequent changeover of staff in critical areas has a huge impact on the effectiveness of any care plan. Despite the commitment and kindness of so many people we have met since Daddy got sick, the reality has often been a painful and lonely experience, for him and for us.

Some of those bad experiences are inevitable. This is a tough situation and may well get worse in the years ahead. The rest? I have learnt that plans can be fantastic, but it's the detail that counts. In many areas the service delivers a great plan but falls short on the detail six months later. And that trying to solve the minor problems that quickly become major crises in the care of a vulnerable person, depends critically on people, people with experience of your particular case.

Getting and keeping the right people in these jobs brings us back to the question of paying more for the work of caring. People who deliver all the complex care the vulnerable and disabled need should be paid more money, but the caring services need to be less about demarcations and petty bureaucracy as well. Care in the community needs to be backed up as well by rapid access to hospitals whenever an emergency arises or, perhaps more importantly, threatens. And communication is the glue that holds it all together, having the right phone numbers often the difference between a problem and a crisis.

There have been funny and happy moments too. A trip to Croke Park to see Dublin play, going to a pub with his sister for a pint, sitting watching the lake outside my sister's garden, his total surprise at the new buildings that have mushroomed around the country each time we go for a long drive—these have all been times when he's happy, when he forgets that he can't move one side of his body. Or when a man who once had so much to say and now finds speech so difficult is able to sing along, word-perfect, to a golden oldie song played on the radio. When he sings again those songs he used to sing at every family gathering and every Sunday morning shaving, then he's happy.

Because it's the little things that make you happy, and it's the little things that hurt the most.

Aine Lawlor co-presents 'Morning Ireland', the morning news programme on RTE Radio 1. She joined the programme in April 1996 and is now one of RTE's most experienced broadcasters as well as one of Ireland's most recognised voices. She is married to Ian Wilson, and they have four children.

Time and freedom

John Leahy

Like most young men growing up in the country, we hadn't much to do, and the idea of a night's drinking was something that didn't seem any harm. Over a period of time drinking caught up with my own life. What I was missing during that time was having gratitude and time for people.

A lot of people put time into me when I was playing hurling under-age and at senior level. I won three all-Ireland medals and look back now and wonder if I valued it enough. There are two tiers to my career as a hurler. The first was when I was out there as a young man enjoying life, having the few drinks and getting into trouble. And then, half way through my career, I was fortunate enough to give up alcohol and really value what sport was about. I now consider myself lucky, even though injury ended my career.

As a young fella I was very quiet, would have stuck to myself an awful lot. I would have known a lot of people but kept my distance. In my last twelve months all I did was drink. I would be in the pub on my own and I had a couple of people I would have been drinking with. I was avoiding responsibility. My job was deteriorating, my sport was deteriorating, I'd lost all my fitness, and I knew deep down that I was very lonely in life and began to think a lot of people did not have time for me. Anger was building up in me, which I put down to frustration, and I did not know where to turn.

The last incident in my drinking life happened in 1996 when I ended up in a cell in Manchester and asking myself, 'God, what has gone on in my life? This is not what John Leahy wanted to do.' The first thing that came to mind was the part alcohol had played. Any time I was in trouble I was drinking. So I thought if I could take alcohol out of my life I'd have some chance.

That was my lowest point, my loneliest. I remember walking round in a circle in the cell and praying and asking God for help. 'Get me out of this one and I won't drink again. I'll live a proper life.'

I told myself that once I got home from England I was going to run to America and let everybody forget about me. People would have known me from the hurling, and lads would be trying to stir it up with me and I'd often be called names, even at work. Some days they would affect me more than others.

I could not sleep that night alone in the cell, and after two nights there I had to go to court, and I remember going into court I had free legal aid and I had a chat with the solicitor. He told me the best he could do was get bail into a hostel in Manchester as it was a gross bodily harm charge and they would remand me to prison rather than let me go home to Ireland. I got bail into a hostel.

My thinking at the time was that I was going to abscond and get out. So I rang a friend and he organised to collect me at the airport. So I was sitting at the airport on the Monday evening, on the run, if you like, and then there was a message on the intercom: 'Could John Leahy please pick up the nearest courtesy phone.' Now I remember thinking the police were aware I was absconding. A good friend of mine was on the phone and told me to get out of the airport as quickly as possible. He said that I should go back to the hostel, otherwise he would meet me and put me on a plane back. If I flew home I'd get twelve months just for leaving.

Another good friend arrived over and booked into a hotel, and it was the first time I could talk about what happened. He gave me time. On the Monday I got bail back to Ireland. Then I realised I had a lot of realities to face up to. Firstly, it made all the national papers back in Ireland. During that previous week I had to ring my parents and my job to tell them what happened.

When I landed in Ireland the following day a friend had arranged for me to go and get help for my drinking, for my life. For the previous twelve months this guy used to ask me, 'John, do you think you're drinking too much?' He obviously saw something that I didn't see.

Then I had to meet the Tipperary County Board. I was playing on the team at the time. The manager of the team was Father Tom Fogarty at the time, a gentleman. There was a couple of incidents they pointed out to me over the past couple of years, and they said if I was prepared to do something for myself they would fully support me.

There were seven or eight people in the room that morning. They all had jobs and they took time off that morning to meet me.

A good friend had organised for me to go to the Aiséirí treatment centre in Cahir for an assessment. I wanted to do it but another side of me just wanted to abscond, go to America and never come back. Then I started to realise that people did care and there were people out there who know what to do.

I left that meeting knowing they were there to support me. Then I went to meet my bosses at the time. I was working for Finches. I was sure they were going to say goodbye and take the car back off me. I met two executives, who were very good to me. There were a few harsh words said and I told them I wanted to do something about it. I apologised for letting them down. They went outside the door and told me they had to be seen to be doing something, so I was suspended from the job without pay for four weeks. I must have been a difficult employee, but they were still prepared to give me an opportunity to get things right. I know well I would have found it very hard to get another job. It was a case of people going out of their way to save a soul or to try and get somebody back on track.

When I think of that journey as I drove up to Thurles and then to Port Laoise, I considered my life was over. My job was gone and I wouldn't be playing hurling any more.

Actually it was the start of people putting time into John Leahy and me putting time into myself. While I considered that night in the cell that this was the end of my life and no-one would want me any more, then the friend who came to me, the county board, my job, and coming back to face the family and the stigma for them. I went into Aiséirí, and they put a lot of time into me and I met people down there, other guys and girls coming from similar backgrounds. It was the first time I had people who understood where you were coming from and you wouldn't be judged.

When I was younger you'd be living up to other families' and other people's expectations. The people in Aiséirí at the time gave me the ability to measure myself by my own expectations. They taught me that I had to get help from other people to stay off alcohol.

A lot of people have come into my life in the twelve years. I got three years of meeting Frank Purcell and the companionship. We'd have the cup of tea, the chat on the Sunday, the cup of coffee. I'd ring him on a Saturday morning and we'd talk about all of life's problems and bounce things off each other. The day Frank died will always stay with me and will always put into perspective the value of somebody's life.

I rang him to meet and I pulled up outside McCarthy's bar in Fethard and rang Frank's phone and it rang out. Then I rang it again and it rang out. And I was right outside the door of the pub, and then a friend rang me about coming to collect the car. And I decided I could talk to Frank later on. But I never got that conversation. It was only at the funeral I realised what type of a person Frank Purcell was. I thought I had a special relationship with him, and I was the only one and I was privileged because we shared a lot, but Frank had that with everybody. He had that gift, the time that Frank wasted with a lot of people. It was probably all taken for granted. Even today I'd walk into the bar and there's a sense of loss.

After leaving treatment my work supported me. I got back into training and hurling again. I played for Tipperary again. I always remember another friend of mine, Johnson Lyons, who was with me the night of the incident in Manchester. I had five or six return trips, and he came on every trip like a body guard. He had a business at the time, a wife and two children, and yet he took time out of his life to stay with me when it would have been easier for him to stand back and not be associated with me.

There was another man, called Paddy Joe, from Roscommon who just rang the operator and got my number after reading about the incident in the paper. I'd never met him but he talked to me for about an hour and a half one night about everything that had happened. I meet him now five or six times a year. He's one great friend that put time aside to ring me. There were letters, good wishes, goodwill out there, telling me to keep my head up and keep going. I've kept them all and look back and read a few of them. They kept me going in what would have been the worst time in my life.

All the great people that have come into my life have given me time and freedom. I will be forever grateful to them.

John Leahy, a former Tipperary hurler, is the holder of many medals, including three all-Ireland medals. He is now a drug education officer with the Health Service Executive in Carlow-Kilkenny. Over the last decade he has toured the country, giving talks on addiction to young people, parents and teachers.

Listening

John Lonergan

In this short article I will concentrate on two separate areas that are central factors when addressing the question 'why waste time on people?'

First of all I will focus on some of the main structures and systems of our society that contribute directly and indirectly to many of the social issues that ultimately cause serious hardship for many people. Secondly, I will highlight how much we all need care at different stages of our lives and why giving time in the service of others is never wasteful.

We live in an era dominated by economics and materialism, when almost everything we do is measured or valued in monetary terms. 'My time is my money' is very much the philosophy underpinning modern society. People are assessed and measured on the basis of 'success' or 'failure', and those who fail to measure up are quickly discarded and given that horrible modern label, 'loser'. Indeed some of the most annoying and frustrating comments uttered all too often nowadays are 'There is no poverty in Ireland any more' and 'If people are poor today it's their own fault.' Such attitudes indicate a serious lack of understanding of how our society operates and how it is structured and also totally ignore the significance of human vulnerability and brokenness.

Recent official figures show that approximately 300,000 people live in consistent poverty in this country. A further breakdown of this figure reveals that one child in every ten is caught in the poverty trap. This is a staggering situation, which will be tackled in a meaningful way only when we all take responsibility and we are willing to contribute generously in providing the resources and support urgently needed to bring about real change.

We can continue indefinitely talking and pontificating about poverty, social inclusion and equality, but nothing will really change unless and until the benefits accruing from our economic growth are distributed overwhelmingly in favour of the poor and socially disadvantaged. At present the reality is that the rich continue to get richer (30,000 millionaires now living in Ireland) while the poor and marginalised continue to lose ground.

The consequences of poverty are numerous and must not be seen in purely financial terms. Two years ago an RTE 'Prime Time' programme dealt with people living in socially disadvantaged communities, and it concluded that every facet of life was affected by poverty. When comparisons were made between children of the middle classes and their peers from disadvantaged areas, the results were depressing. Those living in disadvantage were much more likely to be undernourished, suffer from serious illness or physical injuries, be early school-leavers, be unemployed, have drug and other addictions, be involved in crime, suffer from stress and low self-esteem. For them life is one long struggle.

A good starting point is to get the message across loud and clear that poverty damages people, and that no human being deserves to be afflicted with it. Many people in the wider community are totally oblivious of the appalling conditions many of their fellow human beings live (or exist) in, and they have little or no idea of the huge personal struggles many have in trying to cope with illness, addiction, sexual, physical and mental abuse, homelessness, discrimination, depression, loneliness and many other afflictions.

However, on reflection this is not surprising, as it is a direct consequence of the very divided society we have created. When people have no direct connection or contact with a social issue it is almost inevitable that they will have no real understanding of it. During the past decade, at a time of unprecedented economic growth, the gap between the 'haves' and the 'have nots' has grown at an enormous rate.

At the very hub of this divide is our public housing policy. Building big public housing estates on the outskirts of towns and cities and without many of the most basic services and amenities has created huge alienation and destructive environments where violence, crime and drug use are rampant. Children born into such areas are placed at high risk from birth, and unless and until this fundamental issue is addressed we will continue to pay a big price.

The reason I put such an emphasis on housing is that I believe that if we do not deal with some of the structural causes of alienation the numbers affected will continue to grow and we will never have enough time to give to the normal human needs of our fellow human beings.

Solutions cannot and must not be enforced on those living in disadvantaged communities. We must work with them on a totally equal basis to encourage and support them in their transition. The philosophy of Lao Tsu, from 700 BC, could be a good model.

Go to the people
Live with them
Learn from them
Love them
Start with what they know
Build with what they have
But with the best leaders
When the work is done
The task accomplished
The people will say
'We have done this ourselves.'

Irrespective of who we are or how successful we might be, none of us made it on our own. When we reflect on our own lives we soon realise how much others contributed to our development, achievements and well-being. From the moment of birth and throughout our lives we depend greatly on the care, love, support and assistance of many people: parents, brothers and sisters, teachers, doctors, nurses, neighbours, employers, friends, neighbours, workmates, etc. We must not forget this, and when we are successful we should be humble and grateful for the gifts we got at birth and the opportunities given to us on our way through life.

Few of us would survive for very long totally on our own, and we all need different levels of continuous care, love and support. While some people are far more at risk than others, we are all vulnerable and we never know what is around the corner.

I want to pay a special tribute to those who care for the vulnerable in our society. In modern Ireland their work is often not seen as important or productive, but the poor and vulnerable are the most in need of help, support and, above all, encouragement. Those who care for them, particularly in a voluntary capacity, do so out of a sense of duty and vocation, with no expectations or demands. Serving and befriending vulnerable people is the most noble of all tasks and must be recognised as such.

Over the years, while working in the Prison Service I have met some of the most vulnerable of people. I have no hesitation in saying that the best support one can give is to treat them with respect, be kind and make time for them. Kindness seldom fails. The more vulnerable and desperate we are the more we cherish a gesture of human kindness. Such acts of kindness must not be seen only in materialistic terms. Some of the most profound kindness will centre around words, empathy, understanding, being non-judgemental, recognising the person as a fellow and equal human being, expressing positive and encouraging comments and sometimes, and very importantly, just being with the broken person. Indeed, spending time with a vulnerable person is the most valuable support of all.

We must never believe that it is only the poor or the sick who are in need of support and words of comfort. Throughout our lives we all need the support of others, often just a shoulder to cry on. When one serves a fellow human being, both are enriched and it is often a most humbling and fulfilling experience for both parties.

We must not forget those who work at the coal-face with the marginalised. They understand better than most, and again their value is often overlooked or underestimated. At a recent case conference in the women's prison the discussion dealt with the work prospects of the young woman in question, when a member of the staff working closely with her interjected, 'Never mind work, this woman needs help to dress herself every morning.' This intervention instantly refocused the meeting.

The most powerful of all interaction with our fellow human beings is to *listen*. Allowing people, especially the poor, to tell their story at their own pace and without interruption is the best therapy. It is healing, and it is on such a basis that real friendship and trust is built.

Jean Vanier, that wonderful Frenchman, puts it brilliantly: 'To *listen* another into a condition of disclosure and discovery may be almost the greatest service any human being performs for another.'

John Lonergan is a native of Bansha, Co. Tipperary. He joined the Prison Service in 1968 and was appointed governor of Mountjoy Prison in 1984. He also served as governor of the high-security prison in Port Laoise from 1988 to 1992. He is married and has two grown-up daughters.

The Count of Monte Cristo

Una Lynch

As I write these words we are already more than half way through August in what has been one of the wettest Irish summers ever. To quote a recent commentary on radio from a woman here in the North, the weather this summer has been 'ridiculous.' And yet, despite the unrelenting rain, I, like many others, still live in the hope of blue skies and sunshine.

Hope is a little-understood but hugely powerful motivator. Its capacity to sustain us through difficult times and nurture the human spirit is powerfully captured in Alexandre Dumas's *Count of Monte Cristo*. The young Dantès, having endured almost four years of solitary confinement in a dark and dismal dungeon for a crime that he did not commit, believing that he has been forgotten and is destined to die in his dungeon, resolves to accelerate the process and starve himself to death. On the threshold of death, his life is saved when the 'barely perceptible scratching echoed in his head as it rested against the silent stones.' This barely audible sound, a sign that he was not alone, was enough to rekindle in Dantès the spark of hope and with it the desire to fight for survival.

Dumas's novel is an inspiring study of waiting and hoping. Written in 1844, *The Count of Monte Cristo* also teaches us about the abuse of power and injustice and about the importance of courage, patience and humanity in nurturing the hope necessary for our waiting. Much as I am tempted, this piece is not a critique of the Dumas novel; I will leave that to the reader and will instead reflect on the theme of 'wasting time with people.'

The new Ireland of cappuccinos and designer handbags has increasingly less room for the outsider, for those people who by their very being, hold up a mirror to the underbelly of the Tiger. We are increasingly fed the message that to be happy we must love ourselves; and that love is manifest in the acquisition of things. Therefore people who are materially very poor make us as a society feel very uncomfortable.

Interestingly, though, when people are told that they are dying, priorities usually change and solace is found in the things that money can't buy and in other people. As a nation we are more educated than at any time in our history. And yet even those of us who have borne witness to the simplicity of life's inevitable end get caught up in the trappings of the drama of doing and getting. To absolve the guilt that we feel, we justify the lack of time we have to spend with patients and those we care for by saying how busy we are.

A fiddle-playing farmer and father of twelve children, Eddie Lynch, my paternal grandfather, displayed that innate wisdom so common in the rural Ireland of old. A story that he told is a salutary lesson for today.

A labourer returned to the farm after a hard day's toil in the fields. The horse settled for the evening, the labourer reflected on the day with the farmer. Bending down, he untied one of his boots, and as he took it off he uttered a great sigh of relief and as he shook a pickle of corn from the boot declared: 'That auld thing has been bothering me all day.' Without another word, the farmer went inside, returned with a week's wages, and handing it over he told the labourer not to return.

When I first heard the story my reaction was one of horror—horror that the farmer could be so ruthless. Surely the labourer had done nothing wrong: he was the one who suffered the discomfort, and he hadn't harmed anyone else. Infinitely wiser, the farmer had understood that if the labourer was prepared to suffer unnecessary discomfort and pain all day long, what discomfort might he tolerate for the horse? If the horse was to go lame the entire family would suffer—a risk that he was not prepared to take.

Like the labourer, we tolerate discomfort, pain and hurt daily without question, and in the process desensitise our humanity. The increasing lack of empathy in society and in the provision of health care is symptomatic of our growing tolerance for discomfort. Nursing and medicine were once proudly described as vocations; today we are professions. Governed by the rhetoric of general management, we are driven by targets and performance indicators and imbued with the culture of individualism. The market-driven restructuring of services and efficiency reviews have resulted in a greater demarcation of roles, staff shortages and increased working hours. Not surprisingly, burnout and stress-related illnesses are commonplace. People who are burnt out and stressed cannot care effectively for others, and the first thing that goes is our capacity to listen and to empathise. And listening happens with our eyes as well as our ears.

Eileen O'Neill, a wonderful nurse who died tragically young, recounted her most memorable lesson as a student. 'You feed monkeys; you help patients to eat.' I wonder how she would describe the pathetic sights in beds throughout the island of Ireland today, where even 'feeding' is the exception! It is not unusual to see elderly people, and very ill people, lying flat on their back in bed in 'caring' institutions, gazing in vain at the soggy corn flakes or a rapidly cooling meal that they are unable to reach. By standing idly by or by turning a blind eye to this and other assaults on humanity we are all complicit in allowing these things to happen, and therefore these experiences impoverish each and every one of us.

To be human means to share with others. As illustrated so powerfully in Dantès's tale, we need contact with others to survive. When we accept that progress means less and less time to spend being human, we are complicit in the creation of a society that rejects its most vulnerable. Or, to put it another way, we are complicit in the destruction of society.

We cannot transform a wet summer into a sunny one, but by refusing to tolerate the scarcity of time to share with others we can nurture the hope of reclaiming the humanity at the core of society.

Una Lynch is a nurse and midwife. She has worked in public health—practice, education and policy—in Ireland, Bolivia, the WHO and Copenhagen and has a keen interest in reciprocal learning with partners in the developing world. Her doctoral thesis was 'Public health: Why are the Cubans so successful?' Research interests include public health and the impact of policy on health. In June 2006 Una was appointed research manager with the Changing Ageing Partnership in the Institute of Governance, Queen's University, Belfast.

A morning in TRUST

Geraldine McAuliffe

It's hard to find words to describe a morning in TRUST. When we open the door at 9 a.m., people who have been queuing since early that morning file in. People visiting are often surprised by the relaxed and friendly atmosphere, fresh flowers in the waiting-room, nice paintings on the wall—all connected to our work—and our goldfish, Corky, given to us by a young Cork girl who was homeless. Everything warm and welcoming is our way of ensuring that people feel comfortable.

Sadly, because of increasing numbers and racial tension we have had to make a decision recently to keep our gate shut and allow only so many in at a time.

People arrive with a range of problems, physical, emotional and social. Physical can be anything: gangrene, lacerations, abscesses and, increasingly, blistered and bleeding feet. We patch up as best we can, and what we can't we refer to hospital.

Some of the people who call, live in the hills and parks outside the city centre—many quiet and withdrawn, not anxious to interact with others. Some call with their pets, often excluded from other services. I have a lovely cat at home given to me as a tiny kitten by Kevin, the man who made headlines in September when he died in a skip in Limerick. Eddie, who came to us for years with his three dogs, sadly died in September also, and all of us miss him dearly.

A lot of time is spent liaising on the phone with hospital staff—doctors, nurses, social workers, community welfare officers—indeed people from all sections of the community, including relatives of people who are missing or who have died and increasingly from people looking for advice on how to get help for relatives with mental health problems or how to obtain access to general health services, accommodation etc.

Daily I hear personal and harrowing stories of their lives: families lost because of addictions—drugs, alcohol and gambling; phone calls from people we know in prison just to say 'hello' and 'how is so and so?'

In the last two years we are meeting huge numbers of people coming from abroad, many from EU accession states not entitled to social welfare when they lose their jobs. Recently we had a Lithuanian man who had been working in Wexford. His accommodation came with his work. He was fired unexpectedly, without warning or reason, and subsequently lost his accommodation. He had made his way to Dublin, and when he came to us his feet were bleeding and very sore. He needed daily dressings for two weeks. First he was angry, then he just got very sad.

This is an increasingly common occurrence. One week in September we had people from twelve different countries, most unable to speak English and all like our own Irish who went to Britain or America to work and make money to send home.

People disappear, and you hope they have got out of homelessness. If they have they often don't want to remember where they were. On the other side, daily I am amazed and inspired by the kindness and generosity of people without whom we could not continue. Monthly we give out about five hundred outfits of clothes, all donated to us, as part of a holistic service. Tea and coffee, biscuits, brown bread with lovely real butter and fruit are also given to us by people who take the trouble to bring it to us.

It's a very rewarding job, which I love. Sometimes it's as simple as just getting someone to come back, and then you know you have met some of their needs; other times it's just a smile of recognition. When I'm going home on the Luas I reflect on my day's work. Sometimes I feel satisfied, but there are times when I feel very frustrated at the bureaucracy of the system. When you fall into addiction it's a very chaotic life-style. I can't change anyone, and I don't try to. I accept them as they are and listen to them; I don't have the power to do anything else. I attempt to help and support them as best I can, given the resources available to us. I never feel I am wasting time.

In an ideal world, and if everything was working as we are given to believe, there would be no need for TRUST.

Geraldine McAuliffe, who has Cork roots, is a nurse and is deputy director of TRUST. She is an animal-lover who reminds everyone who crosses her path that animals have a special place in our world.

Maria

Justine McCarthy

She was called Maria, a name that would prove apt. She didn't look Spanish, though she came from Madrid. She was too bubbly to be languid and sultry. She was still effervescing in her lisping Spanish singsong the day after her big date. Her idea of Mr Right was a colleague, tall and ginger with an evergreen bloom of acne, and it was she who had asked him out.

The evening had oozed promise. They had flirted over pizza and strolled back to her flat hand in hand. She was full of imaginings, right up to the moment he formally shook her hand on the doorstep and announced that he would not be going out with her again, because he already had a girl-friend. We adopted a stance of malignant disapproval towards Mr Right after that, despite knowing in our hearts that he had behaved honourably.

One evening his ginger head appeared round the ward door, and we collectively stiffened, making eyes at Maria to signal his presence. She was sitting on the bed with her starched nylon back to the door, munching squares of our friend's Lindt. She spun around and waved a greeting to him of such dead-casual friendship that we felt instantly relieved of the burden of dis-esteem.

Every day that Maria was on duty she came to our friend. She hugged her and exclaimed at her beauty, brushing her hair, eating her chocolate and promising that when she was released from the hospital she would come and visit her in the nursing home. All around, the other nurses whizzed about in a blizzard of snow-white briskness. They changed urine-soaked sheets with swift precision and exhorted their hard-of-hearing charges to walk the corridor with their sticks and frames to regain their mobility. You could see that the nurses worked hard. They had fatigued eyes that never quite saw their patients' faces.

Maria must have driven them berserk, dallying with her girly chit-chat. Every time she arrived, the patient in the bed beside our friend's would detonate with indignation. 'The Irish nurses know how to work, not like these foreigners,' she used to harrumph with the stereo amplification of a deaf person intent on being overheard. It ran off Maria like pouring cream. 'Would you like a drink, Eileen?' she would offer with impervious kindness.

On her days off and after her early shifts Maria would repair to her second job, pulling pints in a city-centre pub. Sometimes she would not finish mopping up the beer spills and stacking chairs until three o'clock in the morning and would have to report back on the ward five hours later. Those days she yawned ravenously, but we never found her sneaking a glance at her watch or gazing past our friend while admiring her elegant pianist's hands or her fine worn skin.

She was ineluctably ordinary. Just a young woman from a big city with a nondescript appearance and a longing for romance. Had we passed her on the street we would not have registered her, for Maria was classically unremarkable in appearance. Under the surface, though, she was extraordinary enough to change the lives of strangers—like us. She threw us and our friend a lifeline to dignity and hope at a time when the resolve to be positive had melted away around us and within us, and she did it with such *joie de vivre* that it never felt as if she was doing us a favour. Her delight in life made her vibrant, and that vibrancy lit up our lives, because she was not selfish with it. The other nurses and the doctors and the social worker showed compassion too, but what made Maria different was that she cared enough to give us her most precious possession: her time.

To me it was no coincidence that her name was the Latin version of Mary, Lazarus's sister's name, the one who grumbled to Jesus that she was doing all the cooking and serving while her younger sister, Martha, sat at his feet, idling. For some reason that parable has always stuck in my head; probably because I grew up in a family of daughters, emerging from the nest with a notorious incapacity for domestic chores. Jesus' admonishment to Mary that she was distracted by inconsequential matters has provided a lifelong licence to steer clear of the kitchen.

We never saw Maria again after the day our friend was discharged. By then she had been transferred upstairs, but she came down to the ward to say goodbye in a whoosh of hugs and promises. She took a last few squares of chocolate and told us her mother was visiting her for a week. She said she planned to take her to an Irish pub and the Phoenix Park and the Guinness museum, to take her mind off the Madrid train bombing.

We were waiting for the lift to take our friend down to the car when Maria said this, and we plied her with supplementary questions. Had she known any of the dead or injured? Did she live in that part of Madrid? Yes, she said, she knew people who were badly injured, and she could have been too. She and her mother had been waiting for a train in the next station when the bomb exploded.

Our last memory of Maria is the split second before the lift doors closed and the whirring mechanism started to take us away from her. There was a dribble of chocolate at the corner of her mouth that enlarged the smile in her eyes.

Justine McCarthy is a journalist with the *Sunday Tribune,* a columnist with the *Irish Independent* and a frequent contributor to radio. She wrote an unofficial biography of Mary McAleese entitled *Mary McAleese: The Outsider* (1999). Her essay 'The making of an Irish Catholic journalist' was published in a collection entitled *Quench Not the Spirit* (2005).

The time is right: The time is now

Inez McCormack

It is well known that in 1954 the US Supreme Court in its historic decision in *Brown v. Board* held that school segregation on the grounds of skin colour was unconstitutional. It is less well appreciated that the court did not set targets and timetables for implementation. When it returned to the remedy in 1955 it mandated change with 'deliberate speed'. The ambiguity in the phrase proved lethal to the hopes of an entire generation of black Americans. Nearly two decades later the majority of public schools in the United States remained segregated and unequal.

The members of the Supreme Court were well aware of the legal maxim that 'justice delayed is justice denied.' Yet they believed that change for black youngsters like Linda Brown could wait.

Change was to be at the time and speed comfortable to those required to change, not at the time and speed of those who needed it. Thus its relation to power and powerlessness defined the value of time.

Linda Brown was eleven when her family's name appeared on the front page of every newspaper in the United States and around the world. Linda Brown and I are of an age. But I was well into adulthood, rather than a child like her, when I began to recognise the need for necessary change in the place where I live.

Challenging those who have power is never easy, and you always need to seek inspiration from the past if you are to shape the future. My own vision was to enable marginalised people to work more effectively to secure a future that enables them to have dignity and respect. That meant learning how to challenge systems of governance—political, managerial, economic or social—that produced the humiliation and invisibility of exclusion.

The means to actualise that vision in a reasonable time frame have evolved over thirty years of working for social change, particularly in Northern Ireland but also internationally. They have been shaped by my experiences in the women's movement and as a human rights, equality and trade union activist. They build upon practical experiences of successes and failures in negotiating with, and not infrequently confronting, sources of power. More significantly, they have come from carving out ways of enabling the dispossessed to be heard.

This required creating new contexts for action based upon asserting their own worth. It entailed crossing many boundaries and creating unusual alliances that affirmed and served the right of such groups to be valued and included. The experience of Linda Brown promised a small step towards a more equal future and simultaneously denied it for want of a timetable, which served to remind me that targets for change are necessary, that a timetable for change is essential, and that the crucial phase is implementation.

This process of implementing necessary change is a slow one. I have always argued that change must be at the speed of those who need it. That argument, either in a work-place in Northern Ireland or in a broader world arena, is invariably met with the doctrine of unripe time: that change is not necessary, not possible, it will cost too much, it is divisive; and when all those specious arguments are overcome, the timetable for implementation remains at the discretion of those who are required to change, not according to the right of those who need the change.

Again and again I was told that 'the time was not right.' Time is generally considered to be implacably neutral. But if, as I was constantly told, the time was not right, that meant that the time was wrong. And if that was so, the people I represented were wrong, part of the problem. We were wasting our time.

So, time was used as a moral weapon—one more means of denying justice, health, education, training, jobs, and access to participation in the decision-making process. Outsiders could have the language of change, but the time would never be right for them to be inside. They might smell change, see it, even touch it, but the time would never come when they could own it.

My own life has been concerned with building strategies to allow that kind of pessimism to be challenged and overcome. In the course of more than thirty years I have undertaken a number of campaigns that have brought me into direct conflict with the powerful. Central to all these campaigns has been finding ways of enabling the excluded to speak for themselves, to challenge and change governance in order that they could participate in the decisions that affect them as a matter of right. I learnt in doing so that it is necessary to challenge effectively what is wrong. But in itself that is not sufficient to make sustainable change. It is necessary to produce 'shapes of right', to work out what systems of governance would look like based on inclusion and right and then to create and build alliances with the dispossessed to argue for them.

Most of my working life as a trade unionist working with poorly paid people, mostly women in the public services, has been concerned with time, power and powerlessness. The workers that I represented included home helps, women who look after frail elderly so that they remain in their own homes, rather than requiring more expensive care in institutional homes. These women cleaned for the elderly, but they also gave of their time to listen to their concerns and worries, or to share a laugh and to cheer them up. The time spent in these human exchanges, affirming the identity and asserting the dignity of those in their care, had a value set at nought by the employers of the home helps. It was costed out. Indeed, on some occasions they were warned not to talk to those they worked for, as this detracted from the time they spent cleaning. Along with these workers, I challenged this view. I argued, without a great deal of success, that the work of the home helps was valuable and should be costed, because it gave a value to the dignity of those they cared for.

In this work I tried to articulate the view that economic relationships should be predicated upon social relationships, and not the other way around; that the values we placed upon social relationships should be reflected in the worth of workers. As my example of home helps showed, this was not some abstract economic argument: it had practical everyday consequences for the workers as well as those they cared for. The lack of value given to the work the home helps did was reflected in cuts in their hours, a reduction of their every activity to the level of the assembly line in Henry Ford's factories. It ultimately reflected a lack of value given to those to whom the home helps devoted their time.

I argued that valuing workers was not only a right way of looking at human relationships but that it was also more economically effective. Cutting the hours of the home helps made it more likely that elderly people would have to be hospitalised. A similar approach to the work of hospital cleaners also reflected a belief that the time they devoted to keeping the wards clean was unimportant. Yet hygiene in a hospital is as essential as the skills of the surgeon or the nurse. The issue of MRSA has demonstrated the validity of this argument. The money required to combat infections in our hospitals is far in excess of that which would allow cleaners the time to carry out the work of keeping the floors clean and the hospitals free from infection. This again stems from a failure to value the human, and a failure to place a value upon time. It ultimately reflects a failure to place a value upon the users of services, the sick, children and the elderly who depend upon care.

Central always to those strategies to assert the value of the time of these workers was their insistence that their change had to be grounded in changing the conditions of those who needed the care.

A result of one of those struggles was a project that I helped initiate in the health service involving employers, unions, workers and users. The consequences of costing out the time and nurture of the women workers in the front line had been so great, in the form of cross-infections, illness and low standards, that employers were persuaded to try an 'innovative' approach. The women at the front line would be involved integrally in discussions on how their work could shape the provision of care. There was little surprise for us in findings that job satisfaction and ill health were directly interrelated, that the strategies of listening and involvement radically changed the patterns of care and reduced infection.

In another part of the project that faced similar problems, the issue was about taking the time to listen to those who looked after the elderly in residential homes. It did matter that the cardigan brought in by the niece when washed in the laundry was then given to someone else, as 'any cardigan will do.' There was a connection between losing weight, getting depressed and being prescribed many expensive medicines because they weren't anybody any more. It is that simple, and that hard. It is about new understandings of what is leadership and recognising that listening and participation have to be grounded in rights, not options, as effective ways of doing business.

For more than thirty years now I have argued for real, measurable change in the North that people can feel, taste and touch in their daily lives. I was one of the founders of a broad-based alliance of workers, sectoral groups and the disadvantaged from both sides of the community in a successful campaign to shape the sections of the Good Friday Agreement concerned with human rights and equality. This resulted in legal and policy requirements on participation to involve those affected in the making, shaping and impact of this change. It has also contributed to an inclusive understanding of equality and human rights as an important element of conflict resolution.

I also learnt in those thirty years that law and policy change realities only when those who need them know about them and how to use them. I now chair a North-South rights project that is concerned with enabling people who experience social injustice and inequality in access to health, education and housing to challenge and change policy and process and to do so by using the tools of right spelt out in the Good Friday Agreement as well as international human rights standards on housing and health on which governments have agreed obligations. The 'best-kept secrets in the world' is how a woman housing activist from north inner-city Dublin described them. The get-out clauses from these obligations are 'when resources permit' and 'progressive realisation'—which simply means once again change according to the timetable of the comfortable.

Part of this work is about enabling residents (mostly women) in some tower blocks in north Belfast that were thrown up in the mid-sixties to challenge the appalling conditions in which they and their children live: pigeon waste on the landings where the children play, sewage coming through the sinks, damp and mould on walls and ceiling. Previous attempts to raise the issues had been dismissed by denying the depth of the problem, blaming the residents for the dirt and never, ever meeting or listening to them about either causes or solutions.

The absence of right is present not just in the daily humiliation of the stink but in the lack of respect of the public authority for the residents: they are housed there because they have no resource and therefore they are worth no resource. Not surprisingly, that lack of value led and leads to depression and self-blame.

In recent months some of these residents, with the support of the project, have set their own indicators of change on these issues, using international housing rights standards. They have set a timetable for those conditions to be changed. They have taken charge of time. They have given evidence to an international hearing based on a survey they carried out that detailed violations of these standards of right. They met the Minister for Housing in a blaze of media publicity to present their case.

Like the cleaners and the carers, the case when made visible is so clear, modest and unanswerable that the minister found it hard to resist and agreed the indicators and timetable for change. The response by the housing authority was to throw money at the problem without listening and talking to the residents to implement the co-operative way forward already agreed with the minister. The result was money wasted and little change.

These residents no longer believe they are the problem and are now insisting that they can be part of making their own change. Time was taken to listen to them, so they are taking their time to assert their value and rights as human beings. They are involving more residents in the campaign and are working with the support of the inter-national panel and local community activists. They are determined not only to change their daily realities but to require that relations between the housing authority and themselves be based on respect and right.

We are at a defining moment on the island of Ireland and in the broader global process. New rules are being written about the practice of political and economic power. The dysfunction between economic and democratic growth at the global and local levels is sustaining dangerous instabilities and maintaining economic and social processes based upon exclusion.

I would argue that the ability as of right to participate in and shape the decisions—economic, social or political—that govern lives deepens our understanding of democratic practice. It is also the key to transforming economic and social relations in a way that is sustainable and stable.

'Participation and active involvement in the determination of one's own destiny is the essence of human dignity' is a quotation from Mary Robinson at a recent conference organised by the Rights Project. It is time that this was the test of all our systems of governance.

Inez McCormack was the first woman to be elected president of the Irish Congress of Trade Unions. She has been active in campaigns for positive action, equal pay and strong equality laws. She is chairperson of the North-South Participation and Rights Project, which enables disadvantaged communities and groups throughout Ireland to obtain access to resources and services through a rights-based approach. She is also senior adviser to the Global Coalition for Women's Rights and Workers' Rights. She was instrumental in the founding of a broadly based alliance of workers, sectoral groups and the disadvantaged from both sides of the community in a successful campaign to shape the sections of the Belfast Agreement concerned with human rights and equality. She has received a number of national and international awards in recognition of her 'outstanding contributions to the causes of human freedom and dignity,' including the Eleanor Roosevelt Award from the City of New York and an honorary doctorate from Queen's University, Belfast.

The outsider

James McCormick

'No man is an island.' We live with and among others. There is a price to be paid for belonging, a price which for the most part we happily ignore. The price is that our behaviour must accord with that which our family or friends regard as acceptable.

Outsiders are outsiders because of rejection of at least some of the values and beliefs of those with whom they are obliged to live. Unacceptable behaviour leads to chastisement, punishment and even death. In our society seriously unacceptable behaviour leads to our being excluded from society by incarceration in either prison or psychiatric hospital, which seems largely a matter of chance, and many will have had experience of both.

The only way in which punishment may be mitigated is by apology, the plea of guilty. 'Mea culpa' leaves the family or wider society secure in the knowledge that their notions of right and acceptable are just and proper.

Those who end up as the 'single homeless', who sleep in the hostels of our big cities or out of doors in all weathers are in this predicament because of their failure to conform to what their friends and families required of them. Outsiders pay a heavy price for exclusion. Most seriously, they are denied the love and support which makes life tolerable for most of us.

Being loved is, I suspect, the best predictor of both a happy and a long life. Those who have been excluded pay the price of forfeiting love, a price paid by both saints and sinners.

In order for us to advance in knowledge and understanding we have to rely on outsiders, those who challenge accepted belief, great outsiders such as Galileo and Charles Darwin. If we remain cabined and confined by family or associates, progress, which demands change, is stultified. This is particularly likely when societies are under threat, as in this circumstance; although they become much more supportive, societies also become much more intolerant.

Our society is intolerant of deviance; we treat our outsiders without respect, without recognising their right to be different. Treating outsiders with respect is at the centre of TRUST's philosophy of care. Long may it continue to be so.

James McCormick was dean of the Faculty of Medicine and Professor of Community Health in Trinity College, Dublin, founding President of the Irish College of General Practitioners, author of many papers and books on medicine, and long-time chairman of TRUST. This article was written in 2003 but has not previously been published.

The language of listening

Rosaleen McDonagh

I shook her hand, recognising the vulnerability in her handshake. Being a professional, I automatically went to take out my pen and paper. I had done this a hundred times with a hundred other women and had rattled off the mantra of safety orders, barring orders and care orders while pretending to be engaging with the women's stories.

I called her a 'client' purely because it created a distance between her life and mine. I had a home and she hadn't; I had a job and she hadn't. I put the box of tissues on the table and took off my wristwatch; these are all signs of power and control I'd learnt from other people too busy to listen to me at a different point in my life. It hadn't registered how complacent and distant I'd become and how conceited my assumptions were. Hidden in my arrogance was an attempt to just get this part of the job over with.

'You probably think all our stories are the same,' she started. The 'us' was a reference to Traveller women. I was stopped in my tracks. My community development training suddenly became redundant. There was no doubt she had ten different opinions about workers like me, just as I thought I'd heard ten different stories like hers.

My phone rang briefly. I looked embarrassed but made sure I checked the message before I turned it off.

'I wasn't always an alcoholic,' she said. 'I know I come here five or six times a year. They think I drink too much. They think I disrupt the system of the refuge. They think I spend my money on too many cans. I've been coming here for the past twelve years. They don't bother asking me what my story is any more. They don't bother asking me if I'm ever going to leave him, or if I'm safe. They stopped taking notes; they just tell me what the rules and regulations are.'

Suddenly I started listening to her voice. I stopped thinking about the meeting I was having after this. This woman's voice was stirring something up inside me—something that was making me ashamed.

'My wedding day,' she started, 'was a big occasion, being the eldest in a family of twelve. My family are wealthy. Yeah,' she said, quite confidently, 'I'm one of the few Travellers who have money.' We both started laughing. 'Well, he has the money, I don't.' There was that knowing nod between women that covers a multitude of things not said aloud.

'It was two days after my seventeenth birthday. The wedding was the talk of Limerick. I thought that marriage was good. I knew nothing better. My mother put up with stuff, but we didn't really see it. We just knew my father was in charge, he was a good man and we loved him. I was his favourite; he never hit me or raised his hand. If he knew where I was now—well, between him and my own children I feel ashamed, like I let myself down.'

During this part of the conversation I took off my glasses and reached for those stupid cheap tissues. Professionals don't cry. I was here to empower this woman. Professionals don't get involved: they go on the journey with the women, supposedly at their pace. But it's no harm to 'jolly' the women along, especially Traveller women. They're not great at making decisions. I didn't want to let a client see me cry, so I made an effort to go to the bathroom.

She touched my hand and said to me, 'You're too soft to be listening to drunken oul'ones like me.'

I wanted to tell her I didn't work for the refuge, I worked for a Traveller organisation. The moment passed; I didn't say anything, I didn't leave the room. I moved my wheelchair away from the table around beside her. I was struggling; her voice was compelling. She was trying to look after *me*.

'The first two years of our marriage we had a great time. He brought me everywhere. We had a fancy trailer and a good van. He spoke to me like he was proud of me and made me feel like I was someone. We socialised a lot. We were the people to know. Or he was the man to know.' We both laughed at this. 'He was good at reading and writing. That's how he got his work. He dealt with settled people, selling furniture, antiques, carpets and stuff. Then the kids start coming, two beautiful twin boys. He was over the moon. I felt I was living a fairytale. Five years on, we had our two sons and a couple of daughters. The girls were my pride and joy.

'When it was ten years into my marriage he shouted the odd time. But that's how men are, isn't it?'

She told me that was how it started. He started talking down to her. She told me she had seen other Traveller men do this to women, and do worse things, and she couldn't understand how they would put up with it. As an outsider you don't know what goes on in a marriage. You're always told that what goes on in a marriage is private business.

She looked at me and said, 'I suppose you think us Pavee women, us Traveller women, are really soft for men. We put up with stuff settled women wouldn't.'

I shrugged my shoulders and felt uncomfortable. I felt a fraud. I wasn't saying who I was or who my people were.

'The first beating happened when he got in trouble with the Guards over something to do with his work. He was raging and just took it out on me. The bruises the first time were hidden under my clothes; he was clever enough not to do it where people could see. We still socialised a lot. He wanted me to look good for him.' She laughed again. 'I wasn't allowed to wear what I wanted. He'd decide what I could wear.

'By this stage, fifteen years into my marriage, our older children were going into their teenage years. The two older lads were turning out to be fine men. They weren't too keen on the business, but I think they were a bit afraid of him, so they went along with whatever he wanted.

'My husband', she went on, 'was always mean and constantly criticising the second fella, Simon. Simon was the quiet one. He had a limp—well, it wasn't quite a limp. One part of his body wasn't right.' She got embarrassed looking at my wheelchair. 'He had some sort of condition, and from the day he was born his father was ashamed of him. To tell you the truth, my husband was irritated with all the trips to the hospital and jealous of the attention my son needed. He used to say, "He needs to be a man like the rest of them." Poor Simon had to try hard to keep up with his brothers. He could walk but not really run.' The tears in her eyes were drawing out the tears in my eyes. 'I think he was like you,' she said. 'But he could walk.'

Silence filled the room.

'I don't mean to insult you,' she said, 'but it's different for Travellers who are not—well, you know, like the rest of us. Simon was a boy, and there was so much expected of him.'

She took my hand. I said, 'What happened?' I had broken the rule of not asking probing or pointed questions. The phrase *The woman will tell you what she wants you to know in her own good time* was ringing around in my head. But we had gone beyond boundaries, and I was glad.

'Remember how I said the kids were in their teenage years? Well, the violence and the bullying were happening every day and every night. Nothing I could do pleased him. Even in bed he would insult me by telling me I was never any good and he could get it anywhere else he wanted it. I knew he was carrying on with some silly settled young-one who was impressed by his money and his nonsense.' She stopped again. 'I'm not insulting settled women.'

I squeezed her hand and I whispered back, 'It's okay if you are.'

She looked at me sharply and was about to question me when I said, 'Go on.'

'You're not writing this down.'

I looked back at her and said, 'You don't really want the barring order, do you?'

She said, 'No, I just want to be listened to and get a bit of peace and quiet for a couple of days. There were rumours my husband had children with settled women. It was my teenage daughters that I felt sorry for; it was awful for them to hear the rumours. It was thrown in their face any time we went to a Traveller do. I was worried we would never get them married because of my own husband's carry-on.

'Twenty years into the marriage now, I'd got used to the broken arms and ribs. Rather than call an ambulance he'd beat me and then put me into the front of the van and make one of the older girls drive me to A&E. He did this because my children would threaten him with the Guards.

'Twenty-five years in he rarely came back to the house. He rarely spoke to me. He just ordered me around and beat me. I was lonely; my children didn't want to be part of the family business. They were all married, and each and every one of them went to England. I know it was to get away from him. The women my boys married were great girls. They put my boys on the right track. They would ring every Sunday, but he would always be there, so I couldn't really talk.

'At this stage my nerves were gone. I was too tired to feel afraid of him any more. I let him do whatever he wanted. Any money I had or any of the money my daughters gave me I spent on drink. Imagine: I was into my forties before I had my first drink, and then I couldn't stop!' We both laughed at this comment. 'My husband was busy rearing his other, settled family. Frequently he told me I was good for nothing and that I was holding him back.

'Then the news came. My son, my beautiful boy of twenty-two, Simon, had taken his own life.'

The room felt small. I didn't know what to say.

'That's when I left the house and the fancy trailer. That's when I started walking the roads and going to hostels. See, he was violent to Simon. Even though Simon took it like a man, all the criticisms that were given to him built up in his head. I thought because he made it out of his teenage years, and he had a wife and a beautiful daughter, I thought it was okay.

'Simon's death hurt more than any beating or anything else my husband ever did to me. At the funeral we didn't even bother sitting as man and wife. By this stage the drink had taken me over and I knew my family were ashamed of me. My daughters felt guilty, but I just wanted them to go away so they wouldn't have to see me or look at me again.

'So this is why I'm here. I'll go walking again in another couple of days and try and get in somewhere else.'

I didn't know what to say. This woman seemed stronger and more honest than me. I asked her stupidly, was there anything she wanted, could I do anything for her.

She smiled and said, 'No, you listened to me, and that's all I really wanted.'

I held her hand. 'I'm a Pavee too,' I blurted out.

We swapped surnames. She smiled and held me in to her. 'Did it happen in your family as well?'

I nodded. I had trained myself to forget about it, just as I had trained myself out of the language of listening. All my education and training made me forget the old ways of listening to someone else's hurt and pain. Everything was for a file or report.

But that's what it's like being a Traveller. You just never know where you're going to have to face another Pavee beoir who makes you listen properly.

Rosaleen McDonagh is a community worker, political activist, academic and playwright. Originally from Co. Sligo, she now lives in Dublin and works as a joint co-ordinator of the Women Against Violence programme at Pavee Point Travellers' Centre.

'Are you happy?'

Patsy McGarry

I t has become a cliché that we are now cash-rich but time-poor in Ireland. I wonder. Perhaps we need to get the Economic and Social Research Institute to investigate that too. Maybe they will find that this is just another myth to be exploded, alongside the one that held that in 'Celtic Tiger' Ireland our rich were getting richer and our poor poorer, while all of us languished in unhappiness.

'Are you happy?' asked that odd Labour Party slogan before the general election last May. It would appear from ESRI findings that, in the main, we are.

But there is no doubt we are busier. It does not mean we have no time. Look, for instance, at the GAA. Is there a more extraordinary example of the success of a volunteer organisation in Ireland today? And I know from family experience how, through winter as well as summer, whole communities are preoccupied with the fate of their local club, whether at football or hurling. The benefits to the mental and physical health of all involved simply cannot be overestimated. What it does for the social lives and morale of communities (especially if they are winning!) is incalculable but wonderful. And no-one should underestimate the contribution of local sport generally to the quality of local life.

Some may demur at volunteerism of that sort, believing, with something of a more puritan edge, 'Oh, that's all right, but what about helping the poor and disadvantaged?'

They might reflect on what that other wonderful voluntary organisation, the St Vincent de Paul Society, does in Ireland. Did you know that it has 9,200 volunteers in 1,000 branches all over this island, and that last year it spent more than €41 million fighting poverty and disadvantage with a wide range of community services?

Or what of the Care Local group in Dublin, which visits vulnerable elderly people in their homes, brings them on tours and organises events and outings for them? It is an example of what so many smaller, unsung voluntary organisations are doing. And while it is always welcoming of volunteers, Care Local, with more than a hundred, has more than its evolving structures can handle at the moment. But demand means it is expanding those structures, so no volunteer is being turned away. Those volunteers, mainly young professional men and women aged between twenty-five and thirty-five (though all ages are welcome), visit an elderly person in their area at least once a week. This generally builds into friendship.

Last year alone Care Local experienced a 60 per cent growth in the number of volunteers, leading to the observation in its annual report, published last June, that 'the popular portrayal of younger people as self-centred and irresponsible does not do justice to very many of them.'

I draw attention to these examples only to demonstrate that the spirit of volunteerism is still alive and well in Ireland, contrary to a perception that would have us believe that we spend most of our non-working lives commuting and are too tired when we get home to be bothered to get involved in anything any more. Not true.

For further proof of this you need only look at all the thousands of people voluntarily involved with school boards and various fund-raising schemes in communities throughout Ireland.

So, in that context, let us look at Alice Leahy's questions about what it would take to make our society a welcoming place for the outsider. 'How can we make more time for what matters?' she asks in a letter, and how 'to make that possible in modern society?' She continues: 'Is it possible any more? Who must show leadership? What can each of us do in our own way to make that change happen?'

First of all, I have to say I am one of those who strongly believe we have handled well the rather extraordinary influx of outsiders into Ireland this past ten to fifteen years. This may be due, at least in part, to our own experience of emigration. Either personally or through family members, there can be few Irish people who do not know what it is to be a stranger in a strange land.

It has helped that over the same period a burgeoning economy supplied enough jobs to accommodate our newer people. Indeed they were here to begin with because such jobs were available, and many will depart, I also believe, when or if those jobs are no longer available.

It has helped too that many of our immigrants are culturally compatible, particularly those from among our largest minority, the British among us, or the next-largest group, the Poles, who also belong to the largest Christian denomination on this island.

Our schools have played a major role when it comes to accommodating our newer people, not least in the Dublin area, where some Catholic schools are dealing with children from countries that number in double digits.

This is not peculiar to urban Ireland. In my home town, Ballaghaderreen, Co. Roscommon, a quarter of the pupils in the local national school are Muslim. They are well-thought-of, highly motivated children, as are the children of the other estimated fourteen nationalities in the school.

But we are still young to this matter of immigration, and this is the time to lay foundations for the increasingly diverse society we are becoming and will remain.

It is where our own cultural attitudes will play a central role. To answer the question, I do believe we remain a welcoming people where the stranger is concerned. But there can be problems. Like language. We must ensure that our immigrants can acquire at least a working knowledge of English through our schools and local Vocational Education Committees.

Education, and media, can also play a role in helping to understand the differing cultural origins and customs of our newer people. These we should strive to accommodate as far as is possible. Towards this latter end we must actively foster, at the official level, a spirit of tolerance and generosity where our immigrants and their ways are concerned. And, indeed, we should foster, equally, an intolerance of intolerance of different ways of life among us.

In this our political parties can play a major role, as can our churches, state and non-governmental agencies. But, ultimately, everyone must be encouraged to do so. And then do so. We must, each of us, actively decide to make our newcomers feel at home. I do not believe that will present any great difficulty where most Irish people are concerned.

While a minority of our newcomers come from backgrounds that do not share a monotheist outlook, the great majority do belong to one of the three great monotheist religions: Judaism, Christianity, or

Islam. Each of those acknowledges Jesus, either as prophet or, where Christianity is concerned, as the son of God.

So I will conclude with an account of a story from the Gospels concerning how we ought to relate to the stranger. It's that of the woman at the well. She was disadvantaged by gender and because she was Samaritan, whose religious beliefs differed from the majority.

She also had quite a marital record!

How Jesus addresses her is an example to us Irishry. And I say that not in a sanctimonious, preachy or religious way, as I am not religious.

In a weekly series for the foreign pages of the *Irish Times* in 2000 I 'rewrote' the Gospels, posing as a reporter in Palestine who was following the itinerant preacher Jesus as he went about his public life. What I attempted was written from what ought to be the usual 'ignorant' disposition of a reporter, i.e. one without any presumption.

No account in that series elicited as warm a response from readers as the report on the woman at the well. Its headline read 'Shared drink at well stirs the waters' and continued:

Judaea, AD 30.—There has been heated debate in Palestine this week following a front-page headline in the *Moon* tabloid on Wednesday: 'Sups with scum: Claims he is Messiah!'

The report, billed as an 'exclusive', concerned an encounter between the preacher Jesus and a Samaritan woman at a drinking place known as 'Jacob's Well.' It is near Sychar on the border between Judaea and Samaria.

At about midday on Monday, Jesus stopped at the well. It is near a plot of ground local people say the Patriarch Jacob gave to his son Joseph.

A Samaritan woman came to get water. Jesus asked her for a drink. She was shocked. She knew Jews despised Samaritans and, besides, she was a woman. 'You're a Jew and I am a Samaritan woman. How can you ask me for a drink just like that?' she asked. He said that if she knew who he was, it was she who would be asking him for a drink instead.

'Everyone who drinks this water will be thirsty again,' he said, pointing to the well, 'but whoever drinks the water I give them will never be thirsty.' She asked for some of that sort of water. He told her to get her husband and come back. 'I have no husband,' she said.

He said he knew. 'The fact is you have had five husbands, and the man you live with now is not your husband either,' he said. She was astounded. How could he possibly know this?

'You are a prophet', she said eventually and, as if to excuse herself and her people, added: 'We worship on this mountain, but you Jews say we should worship in the temple in Jerusalem.'

He reassured her. 'Take no heed,' he said. 'The time is coming when you will worship God neither on this mountain nor in Jerusalem. God is spirit, and his worshippers will worship in spirit. Anywhere.'

But the woman was confused. She was used to worshipping God in one place. 'When the Messiah comes he will explain it to us, I suppose,' she said. And Jesus said: 'I am him.'

At that point his friends returned from Sychar, where they had gone for food. They saw the Samaritan woman but said nothing. She ran off, and in such a hurry that she left her water jar behind.

The friends tried to get Jesus to eat but he wouldn't. They wondered whether he had eaten already. 'No', he said. 'I have food you know nothing about,' he said. 'My food is to do what I was sent to do, and to finish the job.' And they hadn't a clue what he meant.

Just then the Samaritan woman arrived back with a crowd of people from Sychar. 'He told me everything I ever did,' she said, exaggerating in her excitement.

Some of the people spoke to Jesus and asked him to stay with them for a while. He stayed for two days. By then they were saying, as quoted in the *Moon*, 'We believe he really is the Saviour. Not because of anything she said but because we have heard him ourselves.'

The *Moon* report described the woman as 'a slut' and the people from Sychar as 'stupid Samaritan peasants conned by a crazy Nazarene.'

In an editorial on Thursday the *Palestine Times* described the *Moon* headline and report as 'racist, an affront to human rights, and a new low in Palestinian journalism.' It called on the authorities to take immediate action against the tabloid.

A spokesman for the Governor, Mr Pilate, said last night that the *Moon* report and headline 'certainly were inflammatory' but that the matter seemed to have settled down. It was not proposed to take any action, he said.

A spokesman for the High Priest, Dr Caiaphas, said that while such news reports were 'unacceptable' it was not surprising that they should happen in a situation where sects were proliferating all over the country and Messiahs seemed to be 'as plentiful as olives on a tree.'

He condemned Jesus, and for associating with a Samaritan woman. It pained him to use the word 'perverted' when talking about a Jew associating with Samaritans and treating them as equals before God. 'But that is what it is,' he said.

The editor of the *Moon*, James Iscariot jnr, dismissed the *Times* editorial as 'predictable moralising from that quarter. They say their paper's motto is "treating everyone equally", he said, 'and they do. They look down on us all.' He was happy that his own newspaper had lived up to its motto, 'Reflecting the truth as it is.'

Patsy McGarry is from Ballaghaderreen, Co. Roscommon, and has been religious affairs correspondent of the *Irish Times* since 1997. In 1998 he won the Templeton European Religion Writer of the Year award for articles he wrote for that paper. *Christianity,* a collection of essays he edited, was published in 2001, as was *The Book of Jesus Reports,* a contemporary account of the four Gospels he wrote weekly for the *Irish Times* in 2000. In 2006 his book *While Justice Slept: The True Story of Nicky Kelly and the Sallins Train Robbery* was published.

Time

Padraig McManus

If you don't mind, I will begin with a truism: *Tempus fugit.* 'Time flies' is a vexed wail that we utter in a world where many of the occupants spend their time surviving conflict and confrontation, hunger and disease, marginalisation and humiliation, and we, God help us, worry about time's rapid passage and our inability to stop it.

I read that lost yesterday, somewhere between sunrise and sunset, were two golden hours, 'each set with sixty diamond minutes.' But no reward could be offered, as they were irrecoverable, gone for ever.

So when Alice Leahy sent her irremissible request for thoughts on time and how its hasty flight can lead us to exclude the needs of others, the words of the American poet and writer Annie Dillard sprang to mind. How we spend our days is how we spend our lives, she said.

The trick is accepting another, but distorted, maxim: 'Never mind the width: feel the quality.' It is not the length of days that count, it's how we deal with people in the spending of them.

Tragically, it seems that time, that most valuable and irreplaceable commodity, is often the one we are most liable to squander. But, such are the pressures—perceived or otherwise—of life that we believe we don't have enough time to do what we ought.

Reminding ourselves that we should cherish each moment because it will never come again is not the first thought that strikes most of us as we climb out of bed in the morning. It's a principle we rarely, if ever, observe as we rush through the day. Sobering, then, to take stock of Alice's direction and sit for a moment to contemplate how we really do regard time.

Like everything else, isn't it a question of perspective? For the prisoner cooped in a cell, time must seem like an endless burden to bear on a miserable journey. For the homeless person with no house offering shelter and no possessions to protect, the wet day and cold night must be an endurance test to be repeated over and over with crushing sameness.

Conversely, for the greatly privileged among us, time is a commodity in short supply, and we rarely have an excess on our hands. For the better off, co-ordinating time effectively to ensure harmony between work and all the other demands of life is an art that we vainly struggle to perfect. And I suspect that, paradoxically, while modern society has devised multiple and more efficient time-saving devices, those very technologies have become weapons in stealing time from us. Rather than saving our time for better use, these gadgets have enslaved us.

Omni-texting is replacing conversation. Normal tasks are interrupted in order to answer the imperative of e-mail. The Blackberry is now an established tyranny. The shift from what Martin Luther King called the 'person-oriented' society to the 'thing-oriented' society is almost complete; and most damaging—for all the ingenious powers of these mechanical miracles—is their ability to undermine that very first step to communication: listening.

The American philosopher Mark Nepo said that to listen is to 'continually give up all expectation' and to give our attention, completely and freshly, to what is before us, not really knowing what we will hear or what that will mean. 'In the practice of our days, to listen is to lean in, softly, with a willingness to be changed by what we hear,' he said.

In my view, using time effectively can be done only if we listen alertly and hear what we are being told. It is the only way we can hope to effectively respond, to any situation. The measure of really effective management can be found in the value it places on listening to and absorbing the concerns and needs of customers and staff. I think the same applies in all disciplines, especially politics, and to all walks of life, from parenting to teaching to medicine to farming. But listening takes time, and when we believe we do not have enough of that commodity to do as we ought, we fail.

In my everyday experience it impossible to prepare a road map for any course of action without having first listened to those affected by it. But I also know it is part and parcel of our frail human condition that self-interest, as well as time limitation, militates against good listening too.

So when self-interest, or profit, is not served by listening, the time dedicated to the storyteller tends to shorten dramatically. (I don't have a scientifically based survey to hand but I suspect that, in the absence of self-interest being fulfilled, the attention span shrinks to minutes on the part of the listener.) And I think it is here that people who demonstrate to the rest of us how to live life as it should be lived—widening our circle of compassion to embrace a world beyond our own safe and comfortable haven—offer us real hope and indeed inspiration that a better world is possible.

Those who work on the coal-face of need, who never seem to tire of listening to the complex, always sad, often tragic human stories related to them every day, offer us an alternative. Time, the most precious, fleeting thing, they give selflessly. Many of us might not be able to follow in their footsteps, but we can opt to waste even a little more time with others.

Padraig McManus was appointed chief executive of the ESB in July 2002. A former commercial director and managing director of ESB International, he is a fellow of the Institute of Engineers of Ireland and of the Institute of Electrical Engineers. A member of the National Executive of the Irish Business and Employers' Confederation, he is also on the Council of the Irish Management Institute. He is a board member of Business in the Community and a trustee of the US Conference Board.

No time?

Louis MacSherry

Our nation has made huge progress over my lifetime. When I was born, in the 1930s, and through the 1940s and into the 1950s, we were suffering huge unemployment: many had to emigrate to earn an income, and the standard of living in Ireland was not high, with a lot of poverty, particularly in the cities and large towns.

When I was a child it was common to see barefoot children on the streets of our cities. It was a poverty altogether different from the poverty I saw working in Bangladesh in the 1970s—that was a knife-edge existence in which it was a miracle that anyone survived from day to day—and many Irish people have escaped the poverty into which they were born or fell. They did this by their own efforts, with the help of Government policy and as the economy expanded through EEC intervention, improved education for our high population of children and growth in our industries—this last helped by grants and the low costs of living, low taxes for conformations and expansion in the tourist industry. Thus, almost serendipitously, we found ourselves in a position to catch the wave when the technological revolution rolled in.

Today, as we near the end of 2007 and the rate of unemployment is one of the lowest in Europe, our standard of living is high and we have replaced emigrants with immigrants who can make a living in Ireland. We have cars, we have houses, we have universal education, we have a fashion industry, a music industry, a café culture.

But we also have problems we never had before. Our expanding population brought with it a high demand for housing, which multiplied in cost; many people had to move out of town to find a home they could afford—and now they have to commute on roads never meant for this flood of traffic. Sadly, drugs have deluged the country, with the accompanying increase in crime; murders are common. Intolerance and stress are common as people work long hours, commute through gridlocks and face ever-increasing costs and the worries of educating a family to keep up with the high standard of living.

We are gradually moving to Ireland of the Unwelcomes as our stress pushes us to extremes. Many cannot cope with these changes, so we see increases in marriage breakdown, alcoholism, drug abuse and homelessness: beggars are common on the streets of Dublin.

While we recognise the obligation of the Government and other bodies to help those in need at home here in Ireland, it behoves us to act also as individuals too. Since stress can build up every day, it is important that we take action early to avoid such build-up, so that we do not lose the last vestige of cordiality that for so long marked us out as Irish: a smile, a handshake, a ready appreciation of small services—what we used to consider essential politenesses.

Many people appear to fear that if they make any effort to 'get involved' in tackling the problems we face today their already-pressured lives will be hijacked. Well, like so many others, I have been involved with helping organisations in Dublin throughout my life. The amount I have done never took over my life—it rarely even impinged on my family or work lives, or on my social life, or stopped me playing golf or going abroad on holiday (or, indeed, stamped the words 'do-gooder' on my forehead).

I believe that 'getting involved' can be simply a matter of showing that we value those we cross paths with.

Handshakes are a good case in point. Our top Government officials are often photographed shaking hands with other dignitaries; football teams shake hands, rugby teams shake muddy hands. It is a sign of respect. But we all shy away from shaking the hand of the destitute or the beggar. But why? Why do we not take the time—only a few seconds—to restore a little self-worth to those who are fast losing their identity as streams of people choose to ignore them?

'We have no time' is the favourite excuse. It is no excuse. To shake someone's hand takes seconds. You say hello, perhaps you hand over a few coins, you hold out your hand, and you ask after the health and the circumstances of the person you are talking to. This way they are reminded that they are someone with opinions, someone who goes beyond the patch of ground they sit on. They reply, you say goodbye, you walk away.

We have to recognise that, just as we are becoming rich in material terms, we are becoming 'time-poor', even 'time-destitute'. The many things we have acquired make demands on our spare time, just as they bring us satisfaction and pleasure. Far too often we are so time-poor that we have no time to really listen, and we have lost interest in our friends.

And now is the moment to react, on an individual as well as a general level. Before the slump that will follow our boom takes away the means to tackle our new problems, we need to recognise our obligation to value and support all our citizens, even those who cannot contribute to our economy.

This action must be taken by all levels of society: the Government, the corporations, the business community, the schools and parents. Ireland is internationally recognised for helping the underprivileged abroad; we have supported non-government organisations. But our Government needs to give more aid and more status to our home-grown helping organisations. The confederations and private companies could all do more, supporting schools and parents in educating and explaining that many of our fellow-men are destitute and in need of help, oftentimes through no fault of their own.

Louis MacSherry began life as an accountant with Kennedy Crowley, later becoming a management consultant and financial director of various companies. A former rugby player, he now enjoys golf and sailing.

Tear up the time-sheets

Father Peter McVerry

I opened our first hostel in 1979. It was for six young people aged twelve to sixteen from the north inner city. I knew a little about working with young people but absolutely nothing about residential care. Nor did any of the other staff members. There were no courses in child care, no training—nothing. If a kid was causing havoc you just sat on him till he quietened down; if he wouldn't get up in the morning you reefed him out of bed. Nowadays you would be sacked straight away! But it worked in its own way, because of the terrific relationship that existed between the staff and young residents. We made it up as we went along, learning by mistakes, using our gut reaction.

Although we were funded by the health board, the health board neither knew nor cared what we did. The only question they ever asked was 'How many children are living there?' so that they could justify the money they were giving us. Accountability was non-existent.

Residential child care needed to be professionalised, and made accountable, and it was. Vision statements, mission statements, strategic plans, policies for everything (including what to do in the event of a bomb threat!), protocols, procedures, rules and regulations were introduced. Not only must you now do everything correctly (which is reasonable) and be *seen* to do everything correctly (which is reasonable up to a point) but you must *record* that you have done everything correctly (which is a pain in the neck).

Certainly much has been gained by this process of professionalisation and accountability. In that former chaotic, unaccountable world of residential care, some children were abused, some had their rights trampled on, and some were badly damaged by their experience of care. That could not be allowed to continue. But many also found a friendship, a homeliness and a sense of being wanted: their experience of care was perhaps similar to a child's experience of family, warts and all. In the necessary process of professionalisation, the warts are being excised but there is a real danger that the sense of homeliness may also be lost. There is a danger that policies and protocols (necessary as they are) may reduce, or eliminate, the spontaneity (equally necessary) in the relations of staff members with children. The hostel can be so regulated that it may provide a very safe but antiseptic environment for children.

That first hostel was known by children and parents alike as 'Peter's Place', and the children used to say that if they weren't in Peter's Place they would have been in care! We provided a service—admittedly a very inadequate service compared with the services homeless children receive today, but it was more than just a service. Almost thirty years later, I am still in contact with many of those who stayed there.

Perhaps the negative aspect of that change to a more professional service could be symbolised by the use of that horrible word 'clients'. We are now all dealing with 'clients'! We all have a job description, telling us what we are supposed to be doing. We have a time-sheet to fill in. We have a 'work load'. We have to account for how we use our time. The emphasis now is not just on ensuring that nothing will go wrong in our dealings with young people (a very laudable objective) but on making sure that you have followed all the correct procedures so that the blame, if things do go wrong, falls elsewhere. The procedures may become more important than the child.

We still provide a service to the child, and a much better service, but the 'more than just a service' may get lost. Working with people on the margins is fundamentally about developing relationships; slavish adherence to procedures (to avoid the blame if anything goes wrong) may undermine the very work that the procedures are intended to promote. There is a delicate balance between following the procedures that are intended to safeguard the child and taking the risk of giving the child the freedom to take risks.

I used to think that the hardest part of being homeless is having nowhere to sleep, or being cold and hungry during the day, or being bored all day with nothing to do and nowhere to go. But I learnt from homeless people that the hardest part is living with the feeling that you are not wanted, not valued. Those on the margins feel pushed aside, treated as second-class (at best), unwelcome guests at the Celtic

Tiger party. The message they receive, twenty-four hours a day, seven days a week, is that they are just not important enough for this society, wealthy beyond its dreams of just a decade ago, to solve their homelessness. Yes, they want services: somewhere to sleep, something to eat, something to do; but, above all, they want to feel valued.

It is possible to provide beds, food and training—the services they need—in a way that reinforces their feeling of not being valued. If so, it would be better if those services did not exist. While friendship and services are both important, friendship is the most important. We value them by listening to them, discussing with them, being interested in them. We have to choose between seeing them as 'clients' or as friends. No job description can tell us what we should be doing. They are not part of our 'work load'. Time-sheets have to be torn up. We have to give them back the dignity that society, by leaving them homeless, has taken from them. No policies or procedures can tell us how to do that. We can only do it by caring.

Policies and procedures are about efficiency; they are intended to help us to provide a more efficient service. But they cannot tell us how to care more. We may come to confuse providing a more efficient service with caring. But how do you care *more efficiently*?

Homeless people are always on the receiving end of services. 'Clients' are people who are being served. They are being given a bed, provided with food, offered counselling, receiving treatment. They are always getting, getting, getting. But our dignity involves believing that we have something to give, believing that we have a contribution to make to the lives of others, a unique, important contribution. Homeless people who are always receiving have their dignity destroyed in the very receiving—unless they also have an opportunity to give something. And what they have to give is primarily themselves, their story, their experience, the way they think and value and perceive, their unique history, which defines the unique homeless person that they are. And if they are to share this gift with us we have to be able to receive it.

Some have no wish to receive it; some do not see its value; some have nothing but contempt for homeless people. But those who wish to receive that gift that homeless people have to give must have the time to receive it, the time to listen, to hear, to be enthralled, to be shocked—to be shocked sometimes by their history and the failure of our society to respond.

Giving people our time is the greatest service we can give them. And in giving them our time we enable them to take back the dignity that has been stolen from them. Wasting time with them is the greatest thing we can do.

But what on earth would our funders think? The time-sheet they want filled up is blank. We have *achieved* nothing. This is not part of the job description; it is not included in the policies and procedures we are meant to follow. It is just that: a waste of time—and getting paid for it!

But wasting time, just listening, can be time well spent. It can be very demanding, emotionally draining. It can reveal to us our prejudices. It can remind us how fortunate we have been. In listening, we discover part of ourselves in the homeless person who is speaking, because that person, but for the grace of God, could be me: I discover that in judging them I am really judging myself. It reveals to us the uncaring side of this society we live in, and which we have often denied. It challenges us deeply within ourselves. In listening, we are challenged to change; providing services is much safer!

We must certainly provide services to homeless people that are efficient, professional and accountable. We need policies and procedures to protect their rights. But we must not identify this as caring. It is certainly *part* of our caring, but the less important part.

Each of us, homeless person and service provider, has something to give and something to receive. We can become accustomed to giving, while the homeless person can become accustomed to receiving. A service that respects the dignity of those who are homeless is one that allows the homeless person also to give and allows ourselves also to receive.

Father Peter McVerry has been working with Dublin's young homeless people for more than thirty years and has campaigned tirelessly for their rights. In 1979 he opened a hostel to tackle the urgent need for accommodation. Four years later he set up a charity, The Arrupe Society, renamed in 2005 The Peter McVerry Trust, to provide further housing and support. It has progressed from a three-bedroom flat in Ballymun to providing a wide range of services to cater for the diverse needs of young homeless people through supported accommodation, drug detox, and education and training. *The Meaning Is in the Shadows* (2003) is a collection of writings by Father McVerry that reflect on his experiences working in the inner city.

Memories of Miss Harrington

Maurice Manning

One of the calmest people I ever met was Miss Harrington. I never knew her first name. She was of that generation that took a dim view of easy familiarity, and even though I met her five days a week for two years as I dropped my son off to Pembroke Junior School—otherwise known as Miss Meredith's Academy, and as the alma mater of Maeve Binchy—it was always 'Miss Harrington' and 'Mr Manning'. Our encounters did not allow for deep or sustained exchanges, what with the coming and going of parents depositing their noisy children. 'Thank God it's Friday' or 'Not long now till the weekend' or 'The winter is nearly over' tended to cover the range of my contributions. Miss Harrington would invariably respond, 'There you go, wishing away your life. Every day's a good day.'

Pembroke School is no more now, another victim to the property boom of Dublin 4, and Miss Harrington is, I hope, in happy retirement, enjoying her beloved west Cork. But her words remain fresh in my mind and, to tell the truth, have influenced my thinking more than most of the formal and usually gratuitous advice I have been given over the years.

Miss Harrington made me conscious of time. Not so much that we should use it productively or parcel it out into pre-programmed planning—I have had too many people telling me that in various forms and shapes over the years—no, what Miss Harrington was saying was to rejoice in time, to treat all of it, summer, winter, wet or warm, Monday or Friday, as the precious commodity it truly is.

And as I think of Miss Harrington I think also of my old friend Winfred. Winfred and I stayed in the same hall of residence as students in UCD back in the 1960s. Winfred was German. Very German. Conversations with Winfred were not lightly undertaken, unless one had a comprehensive and detailed grasp of all the facts and had well-thought-out positions to steer one through the hard work that a conversation with Winfred entailed. And in those days none of us did have any great grasp of the facts, except maybe on football or horses.

This particular morning I found myself, along with my great friend Andrew Carolan, engaged in a serious—and unsolicited—conversation with Winfred. I think it was about the newfangled Common Market. Then he stopped. Very abruptly. 'I am sorry. I cannot now continue. I am five minutes behind my schedule. If I do not stop now I will be five minutes behind all day. We will this evening continue.' We didn't actually. My evasive skills were very good, even then. But the episode did instil in me a lifelong sense that not all time could or should be so regimented. And that wasting at least some of one's time had a lot to recommend it.

A precept I have had no difficulty in following. But what do we mean by 'wasting'? Some might think that sitting through long, serious meetings is a productive use of one's time. And in my life I have done a lot of it. In my experience the opposite is too often the truth, especially if the outcome is pre-ordained and many of the speeches are merely going through the motions, 'single transferable' speeches one has heard many times before and no doubt will again. So how then to turn that waste of time to advantage?

We all have our own ways of doing it. Over the years I mastered the art of going into a world of my own at such meetings—managing to look serious, nodding at appropriate times but essentially doing my own thing. I managed to write much of my first novel during long meetings of the university governing authority or the endless parliamentary party meetings I was obliged to attend. Nobody ever guessed that I was not taking serious notes of what was being said, or suspected that I might even be enjoying myself.

When talking of wasting time I am reminded of my late grandfather, Ter Nolan of Bagenalstown. Some in his family said he was the laziest man who ever lived. That is almost certainly an exaggeration, but not too much. Certainly he never seemed to work, and certainly he never saw himself as an economic or productive unit. And yet he was the most delightful company I ever knew. He had stories, endless stories of the political battles in Co. Carlow at the time of Parnell, and of Parnell's great visit to Bagenalstown in 1891, when the nuns refused to receive him in the convent and the parish priest defied not one but two bishops in his support of Parnell. He had stories of his long time in South Africa in the 1890s, returning from the goldfields with even less money than he had brought out. His stories of life in Bagenalstown, his marvellous yarns about the characters and the families over the generations, were never to be forgotten. Certainly I never did. There was hardly ever a subject upon which he could not speak with authority, and there wasn't a person who didn't relish his company. A wasted life? A waste of his time? I don't know. But his memory certainly persuades me that a strong case can be made for wasting at least some—and maybe more than some—of one's time.

And I think back too on the 'wasted days' spent with the late Pat Lindsay, the best raconteur I have ever known—long days spent in smoky pubs in out-of-the-way places in Connemara. I should have been in my office doing the work I was paid to do, but instead here I was learning from the rich and wise experience of a man who had lived life to the full, getting the odd word in edgeways as he and Dessie Hynes brought back an Ireland that was fast disappearing.

I know that today it is the 'wasted' time I remember and the memories of that 'wasted' time that give me the greatest and most lasting pleasure.

Maurice Manning is president of the Irish Human Rights Commission. He previously lectured in politics in University College, Dublin, and has been visiting professor at the University of Paris (Vincennes) and the University of West Florida. He is a member of the Senate of the National University of Ireland and of the Governing Authority of the National University of Ireland, Dublin, and was a member of the Governing Authority of the European University Institute, Florence. He has written several books on modern Irish politics and one political novel. He was a member of the Oireachtas for twenty-one years, serving in both Dáil Éireann and Seanad Éireann, and was both leader of the Seanad and leader of the opposition there. He was also a member of the New Ireland Forum and of the British Inter-Parliamentary Body.

Loser: an ugly word

Tony Merriman

Union work is all about listening to people and establishing contact. You have to identify individual needs. The group work will always be there, but individual grievances need to be dealt with, otherwise you have people who go home and instead of thinking about work they're worrying about some issue that could be dealt with.

I've argued within SIPTU that the union needs to be more about lobbying and campaigning. With collective bargaining, the days when people took to the streets are gone. But that was how young people got involved. There was the energy of a protest when a union was active and people saw that they could have a voice.

Although many of the issues have changed over the years, people stay the same. It's like school or anything else. People need to be part of a group and need to be recognised from an early age. People need to know they have a worth.

When you say 'wasting time with people' it's not time wasted, it's time invested. You see it with Government policy, where money is thrown at issues instead of having a well-thought-out policy and time spent on the people who need it.

The needs of people in desperation should not have to be met by volunteers. There is a basic lack of leadership if you cannot have an inclusive society.

With the companies I deal with, like An Bord Gáis and the ESB, it was a case in the last ten years of changing the way we did business. We moved away from confrontation to partnership. When the ESB was in a strike situation we became public enemy number 1. There were restrictive practices and years of problems there. But the work-force has gone from more than 15,000 down to 7,500. Without partnership none of it could have been achieved.

I believe that people need work. People need to get up each morning and have a structure in their lives. For an employer a union can be a good thing. It's all about relationships, and you need time for relationships to mature. When they're established, that's when the fear is taken away.

A union is about more than work issues. It is an important support. It happens all the time where people might have addiction or psychiatric problems; a union maintains the link and you maintain the employment when companies are not found wanting. A good number of people recover, and their future is safeguarded.

The sense of belonging has changed in Ireland, as has the tolerance in Irish society for the loner or the outsider. Peer pressure and the act of bullying have increased, not only in the work-place. Sometimes people have everything, but because time hasn't been spent on them by family or friends they take out their anger by becoming bullies. Affluence does not always lead to good relationships. In all walks of life I think we need to respect each other and be mindful of confidentiality and always question and look at our own attitudes.

Investment in support for families and schools could carve pathways to the future for people who would otherwise fall through the gaps. The professionals need to listen to what parents and children are saying. I can look at groups of five-year-olds and pick out the kids who will be in trouble later in life. You need the intervention in families where there is no tradition of education. And it's a question of time, not just money or resources.

I notice a change in parents' attitudes, where competition is being encouraged too early. I once saw a father strike his nine-year-old at a football game because he didn't think he had played well enough. We have five, seven and nine-a-side games for technical development to train the children. But this pressure from parents and different clubs has turned them into cup competitions, with leagues and trophies. Instead of becoming development games they become competitive games, and eight-year-olds are screaming and roaring at the side of the pitch.

Development is about learning, not winning. Kids are competitive enough, and they don't need extra encouragement. You hear that American term a lot these days: 'Loser,' they say. It's an ugly word.

Tony Merriman is a full-time trade unionist with SIPTU. He is a worker-director on the board of the ESB and a member of ESB Electric Aid. From Crumlin in Dublin, he joined the ESB at the age of eighteen, having already had two years' experience as a shop steward in his first job. He is involved in community and drug prevention projects and is chairman of Lourdes Celtic Football Club, which has up to five hundred players between the ages of five and nineteen.

The Coffee Club

Vinny Murphy

Frank Purcell, one of the men to whom this book is dedicated, was a member of what he referred to as the Coffee Club. The club has thousands if not millions of members all over the world. Some join for life, some for a while, and some come and go. But all the members have one thing in common: they all want a life without alcohol.

Frank was one of the very lucky ones. He was able to stay off the drink once he gave it up. And in his own quiet way he was able to help others in the club if they were in danger of falling back into the habit. As a busy businessman, his mobile phone was always ringing. And, like most of us, he didn't always answer it if he didn't want to talk to someone at that particular time. But some people always got an answer. 'I have to take this call' often meant that somebody was in trouble. He would then disappear out into the garden or off in the car. His few words of reassurance might just be enough to keep a friend off the bottle.

That said, he loved the buzz of the bar. Which was just as well, really, as he met Annette, who owns McCarthy's Bar in Fethard. Frank and herself both got a second chance after failed marriages and fell in love. He didn't demonise pubs, publicans or drink just because he couldn't have a drink. In fact he was just as likely to be in the middle of a sing-song in the bar as the fellow who had been drinking there all day. As I said, he was one of the lucky ones.

One quiet night Alice Leahy and her husband, Charlie, walked into the bar. 'I know that woman,' Frank said, trying to place her face. Frank, like Alice, had left Fethard many years ago. I refreshed his memory. 'Ah, I know her now,' he said, and off he went up the bar to chat to Alice and Charlie. It was the first of many chats and the start of a special friendship.

Later that night, when we were cleaning up the bar, Frank approached me. 'We'll have to do something for TRUST. A lot of the people in the Coffee Club are friends of TRUST. I sat in on meetings with many of them over the years' (meaning AA meetings). 'She's the only good thing in some of their lives . . . Tell you what: we'll start a golf classic!'

It was formed there and then. It went well. We raised €8,000 in the first classic. Each year it got better. Then, one dark night, Frank dropped dead. He had had a massive heart attack.

His friends arrived from all walks of life for his funeral. Many were members of the Coffee Club. Many others were from the world of sport: he was involved in motor racing and horse racing and passionate about Tipperary hurling, a passion he shared with his lifelong friend Babs Keating, who gave a wonderful oration at the meal after we placed Frank in his final resting-place in the soil of Co. Tipperary.

That night we renamed the TRUST Golf Classic: it became the Frank Purcell Memorial Golf Classic in aid of TRUST. And his friends made a commitment to help. So far we have raised €80,000 for TRUST; this year we hope to break the €100,000 mark. It's a fitting tribute to the man who gave so much of his time to others.

Vincent (Jasper) Murphy is joint founder of the Frank Purcell Memorial Golf Classic in aid of TRUST. He runs McCarthy's Bar in Alice Leahy's home town of Fethard, Co. Tipperary, a family business that comprises a bar, a restaurant, and an undertaker's. He is married to Sarah, a native of New Zealand. They have two daughters. A graduate of the National University of Ireland, he is at present researching the life of a Fethard man, Vice-Admiral Henry Kellett. In his spare time he likes to write, travel, play music and fly.

French time

David Norris

I am not really sure that I think it's that easy to waste time. After all, time exists outside and independently of us. What we can do, of course, is live life at various levels of intensity. In fact a lot of the things that are commonly described as wasting time seem to be fairly enriching.

My downstairs tenants, for example, have done a wonderful job in our little garden in North Great George's Street, and I now often take my breakfast out in the midst of their handiwork. I read the newspaper, drink my coffee, crumble the last remnants of my toast and feed it to the little family of robins while listening to Lyric FM on my earphones. To some people this would be a waste of time. For me it's what life is all about.

I have to say I am all on the side of the French in this (or at least the French before Sarkozy). They have been widely criticised for their adherence to the ideal of the 35-hour week. Apparently this goes against the Gradgrind economic theories of the European Union. But isn't that part of the charm of French life: that they actually will take half a day off and have a long, leisurely lunch with good wine under the trees with their family. That, in my opinion, is what civilisation is all about.

There is such a hustle and bustle about modern life that I sometimes wonder if too many people aren't pushing themselves very hard in order to achieve what they see as their ultimate goal of success in material terms, when they suddenly realise that life has in fact passed them by. Or else they literally work themselves to death, slaving away, denying themselves innocent recreation, and collect their gold watch at the retirement party, only to drop dead three weeks later. Hardly worth it, is it? I am rather inclined to agree with the poet who said memorably, 'A poor life this if, full of care, we have no time to stand and stare.' I am a kind of professional stopper and starer, and it was partly thanks to my fascination at gawking in through people's lighted drawing-room windows that I managed to get my house in North Great George's Street, so that ain't bad, is it?

When I was young my grandmother lived with us, and I adored her, but she was a stern Victorian moralist, and I still live in the over-hang of some of her puritan precepts. She certainly believed it was possible to waste time. In fact she often pointed out the corner-boys in the poorer parts of Dublin who made a habit of lounging about and speculated on the futility of their existence. I hope it didn't seem futile to them. That is the real misery, if by moral bullying you are made to feel that your life is futile. That is why I hate those expressions 'So-and-so is a waste of time' or 'a waste of space.' Properly considered, no-one is a waste of either time, space or effort.

I know the guilty conscience that comes from childhood memories of such phrases as 'The Devil makes work for idle hands' and 'I wasted time, and now doth time waste me,' but I'm damned if I am going to feel guilt about sitting up on the roof watching the two families of sea-gulls nurturing their chicks between the chimney stacks while puffy white clouds file slowly past the distant blue of the Dublin Mountains.

On the other hand, other people can waste your time for you. A notable instance is the banks. As we know, the banks don't like customers unless they are big corporate concerns; that is why they try to discourage us from entering their premises and keep us at bay with the use of computerised plastic cards and punish us by deliberate enormous queues at the 20 per cent of cash positions that are open at any one time.

There is also the horror of official bureaucracy, especially in the immigration area. I listened with astonishment the other day to Melanie Verwoerd, former ambassador of South Africa to Ireland, detailing the delays, the procrastinations, the dumb insolence with which she was met when she tried to get her documents in order. That, of course, could be construed as a real waste of time in the personal sense, although it did have the positive effect of incensing Mrs Verwoerd to such an extent she actually went on the radio to complain. And bully for her! That could hardly be described as a waste of time.

These tactics, of course, are deliberate attempts to keep the public at bay; but just as bad is the so-called Irish sense of time, under which people say they will meet you at six and turn up at seven quite nonchalantly. What they are actually saying, or implying by their actions, is that their time is more valuable than yours, and naturally very few of us feel that this is the case.

I do, of course, know all those phrases about spending time 'constructively'. In American business-speak this means that there should be 'product' at the end of any given period. But what does that do to our social relationships? Spending time with friends or family is scarcely a wasting of time. In fact I think it is quite difficult to consider spending time with other people, however apparently trivial the interchange, as a waste of time.

I lived with my aunt for several years in her nineties, and then she went into a very nice old ladies' home run by the old girls of Alexandra College. I used to visit her every day. I felt it was important to do so, and I enjoyed and was enriched by these experiences. They were obviously very important to her too, as she looked forward to these visits and noted them eagerly in her diary. However, because she spent so much time on her own she was hungry for conversation. If I came in tired on my way home from work and sat down to take my breath she would often say, 'Well, have you come here just to sit and gasp? I'd like a little bit of intelligent conversation, please.' After she died I found that she sometimes noted: 'David was in today for a short time.' Of course, one or even two hours in a 24-hour stretch is not that much if you are on your own for most of the rest of it; but it is still quite a bite out of an active life on the part of the visitor.

Wasting time can actually be quite a useful technique in some circumstances. It helps us to avoid or postpone chores for which we are not quite ready. How often when preparing an article like this have I started off by sharpening 57 pencils, throwing all the tea towels into the washing-machine or sorting out the spoons in their little drawer! This allows the ideas to marinate in the old skull until they are ready to emerge at last.

In fact I have a confession to make: preparatory to writing this little piece I decided I simply had to reply to all those charity requests for money that lay idly at the bottom of my briefcase for the last week or so. This satisfactorily done, I popped across the road to the post box and bumped into my good friend and neighbour Eddie Kenny.

There was another half an hour gone. That was a lucky escape. I remember one time when I had a visitor from the North, we were going to go out to the cinema but we met Eddie on the doorstep, and he came in for a cup of tea. It was six hours later when we realised the time was fled. But was it wasted? I hardly think so. We had had a mammoth one-man comedy entertainment by one of Dublin's greatest raconteurs. I will tell you something. I didn't feel the slightest damn bit guilty about it.

David Norris is a member of Seanad Éireann and of the Joint Oireachtas Committee on Foreign Affairs, a founding member of the North Great George's Street Preservation Society and the James Joyce Cultural Centre, and a campaigner for homosexual law reform.

A new baby

Bernie O'Callaghan

Each one of us has our own birth story. I am really lucky in my work, in that I attend many different births, some in a hospital setting, some at home. Does the way we are welcomed into the world affect us for the rest of our lives? Perhaps it does.

Researchers tell us of the importance of loving human contact from a main carer in early-childhood development. All of us have a natural instinct to comfort a crying baby.

Since the beginning of time the process of conceiving a child has not changed, and the process of giving birth hasn't either. Some babies come gliding into the world and others have a slow and troublesome passage. No two births are the same—how could they be, when no two people are!

The past few years have seen big changes in Ireland, with many people from overseas making this country their home. This brings challenges in the way we communicate with them and care for them as they start their families. I can never imagine giving birth in a country where I didn't speak the language or hadn't built up a good support system for myself. Yet this is now happening all the time for women.

We communicate so much with our body language and tones of voice that it is possible to establish or even change the ambient atmosphere in a birthing situation without any relevant vocabulary; but it is not always easy.

Each birth brings with it the unique story of the mother's life experience, and respect for that is essential. Imagine a family living in just one room. Mother and father already have a toddler and now a new baby. There are fifteen other people living in the house. Yet in their country of origin it would not have been possible to even imagine having two children. They are overjoyed.

To be separated from your own child is a terrible thing; it goes against maternal instinct. Imagine the mother whose husband and other child are thousands of miles away while she is the breadwinner here in our booming economy. She lives in a room in a house with twelve other people. She has a new baby. She is all alone.

When I was growing up, a favourite question of my dad's was 'What do you do in your spare time?' Mostly this was asked of my school or student friends, so they understood the concept. Spare time was something they had! Nowadays I am not as aware of having much of it; but where has it gone?

One winter I spent a week in the frozen landscape of northern Finland. It was −45°. Time has never gone so slowly for me, and I was delighted when some local mothers arranged a craft class. We spent a whole day making robins out of wool and beads. Was I delighted they chose to waste their time with me? Yes! The robins went onto our Christmas tree for years!

'Wasting time with people' is a contradiction in terms. Time spent with people is never time wasted.

Bernie O'Callaghan is a wife, a mother and a midwife. She lives with her family in Dublin and works in the National Maternity Hospital community team in Co. Dublin and Co. Wicklow.

'Eyeless in Gaza at the mill with slaves' [MILTON]

Marie-Louise O'Donnell

There was a woman on the radio the other day. It could have been any day. A specialist, a panellist, a sayist, an opinionist, a teller of the way it is-ist, someone who knew a lot about business or was successful and very profitable in some form of business.

Why else would she be there? Why is anybody anywhere of significance unless they are successful in business, know the monetary way forward, and have their clever financial finger on the profit pulse? Is it not the successful in business and indeed in the business and finance of politics, organisations, management, media, papers, banks, shopping centres—not to forget the Law Library—who have the only opinions worth listening to? Ever heard an old teacher or an old social worker telling you anything on the radio or the television? I haven't, and I listen every day . . . But back to the conversation.

This large and great panel were having even larger and greater and, more importantly, inspired conversations about the country's everlasting tribunals. We could sing it as a country-and-western tune now:

Should they stay or should they go?
Some felt yes, some felt no.
Some said high, and some said low,
But I just stayed outside . . .

We're all so tired of the tribunals, are we not? Despite the decades, rhyming couplets are just not enough to keep us interested.

Our business and financial specialist summed it all up. She had the real and purposeful insight into it all. What she thought, and what she said, mirrored a simple everything about us as a society in Ireland in 2007. She felt that the tribunals should be scrapped. They were costing too much money.

Enough money spent was enough money spent. They could no longer be justified. We should act with sense and surety, assess this cost realistically, and they should cease immediately. Everybody agreed. A chorus of approval. Marvellous!

But what was she really saying? I'll tell you. She was saying that the truth, its searching, its finding, and its airing, is really too expensive. We need to get real, organise ourselves, and stop wasting unnecessary taxpayers' money on it.

We can go ahead and produce certain truths if they fall between the acceptable rationality of the economic graph. If truth or the idea of it falls outside these boundaries or parameters, one of the richest countries in the west will find it just too expensive or just too difficult to manage. Trying to get to the bottom of it cannot and should not be justified.

Imagine that. The truth is now to be measured and decided financially.

However, if you have enough money you can depend on us to find the truth—indeed we might even get the whole truth. Not enough money, you're sunk, and you might as well forget it, or better still make it up, or live in the half light. Enough money spent means that we have enough truth learnt.

The idea of the truth will now reside in truth banks, alongside all the other necessary real truths, like profit, profit, credit and profit (sounds like a law firm). It will be found in the shadow of the coin and the note, the Dow and the NASDAQ, the Mastercard and the American Express,

found only where the shadows sign
in the lift and in the shine
of the profit margin line.

That could be another country-and-western song.

Truth will have the same value, worth, and not to forget colour, as the greenback. Truth will be profitable or it will not be profitable. Finance, financial foundations and financial processes will be a whole lot more convenient.

People are just so inconvenient. They cost a lot of money and they take up far too much time and definitely far too much room. There has to be another, more efficient way to breathe. And there is.

What we are now getting sucked into is the ludicrous belief in a life force that resides with the monetary expert, the research expert, the theory expert, who all live in the comfortable world and the market world of statistics, quantitative research, monetary value, performance indicators, benchmarks, cost-effectiveness, clients, inmates, best practice, economic graphs, policies and agendas. This has now become the acceptable language of who we really are, and how we define ourselves, how we live and what we are to expect of our living days, depending for life-meaning on economic rationality and submitting always, without a fight, to the values and the truths of the economy.

The six o'clock news is led by histrionic music, grave faces, lowered tones. The dawn of the end! The war of the worlds! The terrifying, gulping news from the index-linked central bank stock exchange tsunami is upon us! What's to be done? The central banks have spoken. The dollared god has pronounced. The interest rates are up. There will be grave and deathly cuts in our spending. We are sunk!

We are sunk, and the outsider on the corner against the wall will be the first victim, and whether the tide is in or out he will be sacrificed on the altar of Bureaucracy, whose crest is always the financial template.

The gods of Bureaucracy are alive, adored, and nourished in all our institutions, universities, organisations, political structures, county and city councils, spending ministries and public and private banks. They also live locally, regionally and nationally in infrastructure, architecture, religion, leisure, natural resources and even graveyards. They have huge offices, and, like Parnassus, every road and all decisions, ideas and knees bend and lead towards their policies and ideals.

Their power is in their libraries of theories, theses, reports, manifestos, analysis, research outcomes—all muddled and mushed in meaningless jargon, leather-bound and high-shelved. Their language of policy and value is an insurance against the wind of the world where real things happen.

These bureaucratic gods create diktats about how we can live. They commission studies into who we are, how we are, where we are, and how we have got to where we are. They research into our futures, propelling us the best way forward. Their best way forward.

But creative and imaginative ideas or solutions cannot get into this space, passion is not considered to have the right kind of intelligence and remains usually alone and outside. The inspired personalities ignore the queue, are considered mavericks and possessed only of inconvenient truths. They usually also stay away. Knowledge gleaned from those who work at the cliff's edge has no priority. Those who want to submit to the value of passion, creativity and imagination or to the belief in the human being above that of the policy have nowhere to go.

Does anybody know where our sense of the ordinary has gone? Our sense of what we know instinctively and intuitively—why has that no voice?

It is only if you are extraordinary that you are recognised. But extraordinary at what and extraordinary to whom?

I'll tell you. The extraordinariness of the vulgar, self-propelling and promoting personalities. The extraordinariness of the flaunting of wealth and the success of material privilege. The getting noticed and admired for nothing and no reason. Let's join in the collective silence, let's allow the televised extraordinary, the beautiful, the wealthy, the celebrated, the materially successful to veil and cloud our civic virtue. Has this become the only way to be heard or be human?

The ordinary who live out their lives in the Third World here in Ireland are trotted out on radio and television not as individuals who have something to tell or teach us, some personal narrative that just might make us think again or differently about the way we construct our world, but as visual and aural aids for the comfortable, the extraordinary and the recognised to marvel at their tenacity, grace and grit. And to have us thank God in our own hearts and heads that it is not us who face the daily challenge of being other.

When my father was dying in the Blackrock Hospice I would have robbed every bank in south Dublin to save him. But no money could untumour his lungs and prolong his life. The carriage of death had no interest in financial or bureaucratic strategies. The only thing that really saved him on this alone, silent and personal journey, and saved me in the traffic of the living world, was our human connection, our everyday conversation, feeling, look, history, texture, skin, smell, touch and love. The human-beingness of us both. The comedy and the tragedy of breath and breathing, face and form, existing and leaving. Yeats's 'rag and bone shop of the heart.'

What do we know of the actual living and breathing and loving lives of the individuals who are 'eyeless in Gaza at the mill with slaves'? What do we know of their seasons? What do we know of their 'where to lie down tonight' lives? What do we know about them? The wanderer in huge coat with dropped head, the matted-haired plastic-bagged lady, the weathered drunk and the hollowed-out drug addict? Where is the research for that?

I'll tell you where we think it is. It's in the blaming of the victim, the outcast, the lost. They surely are responsible for their own misfortune. Let's avoid them, walk away, isolate them. They made their own outdoor mattresses, let them sleep on them.

What do the gods of research and bureaucracy know of this? And if they did begin to know something of it, how would they calculate and inculcate this knowledge into their reports, test, texts, surveys and findings? How can the gods of research and bureaucracy restore dignity and respect to the individuals who become the city walkers, the benchers and the doorway sleepers? Could we design an emotional and touch statistic for that?

Why are thousands of hours of desk time, and thousands of trees of paper, and thousands of euros, spent on what we already know? Why do we allow bureaucratic and financial measurements and policies that only serve to undermine and close us down as human beings to be our method of informing our consciousness?

Why are we choking, choking, choking from information and dying from a lack of the oxygen of action? Why do we wallpaper, tongue-and-groove and sculpt our island with reports and surveys and ignore our own breathing reality and the reality of others?

How much research do you need to know, and how many documents do you need to write, and how many reports do you need to bind and shelve, to understand that hundreds of people of all ages, creeds and classes sleep on the streets? That they have nowhere to go all day, are disconnected, dispossessed, disavowed, disallowed, and are moved on, or up, or around corners, as long as they just stay out of the way?

How much more research do we need to do to know that people who work on the ground with the old, the unheard, the tired, the useless, the unwanted, the unlived, the unloved, the unwashed, the untidy, the unclean, the unseen and the vacant are the real leaders, the serious and passionate purveyors of political inspiration?

Is it too difficult for our set-up of systems to really know and fundamentally understand what is going on? We do not really want to pay to get to the core of the problem. It is far more convenient to let the research do the work, and let the research decide on the outcome, even though a child could tell you what should be done to begin that fundamental change.

We are all now among the new intelligentsia: individuals, capable individuals, extraordinary individuals, who believe in the power and the continuance of our own individual independence. Another chorus of approval. Marvellous!

Nothing could be further from the truth. None of us are independent. We are all a product of our connections with our past and present, and with our future. We are all interdependent, connected by heart, breath and tongue, thinking and feeling, to all who cross our living path.

When a citizen gets caught in the chaos and the contradictions of policy versus people, policy will always win. When a carer, a social worker, a counsellor, a youth leader, a nurse, a teacher, find themselves set against the agents of the state, the technocrats, the bureaucracy and the spending ministries, they will lose. Have no doubt, they will lose.

Why? Because of the truth of what money dictates, because of the financial difficulties with these kinds of truths, because of the inconvenience of people, because of the lack of collective responsibility, and because what we are beginning to realise and feel in Ireland is a subtle withdrawal of the state as the guardian of public interest, in favour of the leather chairs at the directors' meetings in world banks.

Society has only ever asked me about my material contributions. 'What do you have?' they ask me. 'What do you need?' is never asked. It has never asked me what my commitment or my enthusiasm is, or how I might like to use it or be facilitated in that use. I know of very few, if any, institutions (including educational ones) that might begin to ask these questions.

People talk about breaking silences. I should like to suggest that we silence noise. The noise of the political, institutional and organisational bureaucracy that replaces living, passionate, creative, visionary, human ideas with costs and balance sheets. The noise of professionalism and expertise that finds its reason for living in being experts on paper and in theories, roaring the loudest through the polygraphs, the surveys and the theses like a Mystic Meg, proffering the right and only life way forward—a path that is usually galactic light-years away from the fragile and sometimes wretched human condition. The noise of the modern, which has made us more backward as humans and reduced us to the will of the policy and the administrative process. And finally the incessant and unrelenting noise of economic rationality, offering up daily the pulse and blood pressure of budgetary restrictions, which by their very nature cannot and will never allow us to have the hope of living as joyous and spontaneous human beings.

Change starts in hearts and minds. Not in thick wallets. Not in world banks. Not in big budgets. It starts with you and me. That we must never forget.

Marie-Louise O'Donnell studied at the University of Nottingham, NUI, Maynooth, UCD and the Guildhall School of Music and Drama in London and became head of drama at Our Lady of Mercy (Carysfort) Teacher Training College, Blackrock, Co. Dublin. She trained as an actor and theatre director and in radio drama production and presentation with BBC Radio 4 and made and presented radio programmes for several years. In 2000 she toured with the acclaimed Northern Broadsides in Shakespeare's *The Merry Wives of Windsor* and *King John*. She initiated and directed The Arts at Dublin City University, creating a platform for Pimlico Opera, the Royal Shakespeare, the Ford Society Awards, Children's Arts Days, Dublin Weekend Radio, the Wild Space Theatre and the Writer in Residence series. She began and developed the Larkin Concert Series in north Dublin and was part of the team that imagined, built and launched The Helix and programmed Theatre Arts there for three years. She developed and artistically programmed the Space theatre and created Fizzfest, a yearly theatre festival for children. She recently returned to the School of Communications in DCU to lecture on the art and craft of radio and on cultural performance.

Forgotten treasure

Fergus O'Ferrall

'*For where your treasure is, there will your heart be also*' (Matthew 6:21). In Matthew's Gospel, Jesus underlines a central principle of our lives: our hearts will be focused on, and our energies directed towards, that which we consider most important in life—that which we treasure.

In our busy, frenetic lives we moan about not having 'quality' time to spend with other people, even with our families. If we are honest with ourselves we will admit to 'making time' for those things that we do in fact treasure. People in every age and time forget where their 'true' treasure lies: the psalmist accurately saw that we are a people 'that do err in their hearts.' The heart of humankind is indeed 'astray' (Psalm 95:10) and never more so than in Celtic-Tiger Ireland.

We have been so busy laying up for ourselves 'treasures upon earth' that we have hollowed out of our health and social care systems the character of care that is essential to curing the dis-ease that afflicts so many in our greedy, materialist, individualistic and selfish culture.

The counsel of Jesus appears at first to be naïve, but upon reflection it is profoundly subversive of our current political and social outlook. It is countercultural, because to have the courage to put into practice, against the prevailing system, caring as a central activity will in turn breed amongst health-care staff caring as a renewed professional commitment, and this in turn will eventually seed a new kind of politics that truly values caring for people when they are vulnerable. This indeed may be the only way to stop the erosion of the ethic of care in our society.

Many of us who have absorbed the false idols of neo-liberalism from the 1980s onwards will have to learn again what it means to care

for other people; the characteristics of caring have to be freshly articu-
lated, as our medical and indeed nursing professions have to a great
extent lost the art of caring; also the character of the carer has to be
re-expressed at a time when the personal attributes of the carer have
been seen as less important than technical proficiency.

Caring means trying to feel one's way into the experience of
another so that one is able to do for the other what they would wish
to do for themselves, were they able either physically or mentally so to
do, and to care in such a way as to cause the cared-for person's sense
of wellbeing to be enhanced. It is fundamentally a relationship of love
and often requires a lavish expenditure of time.

Such caring is fragile, because it requires putting other pressures
aside and focusing on feelings, listening, relinquishing judgement
and prejudice and making a commitment of time and energy to a
relationship. Such caring often cannot survive within an organisation
that is measured only for 'value for money' or financial efficiency.

Imagine a common hospital ward scene. A flock of white coats
hovers above a young man in a hospital bed. The consultant tells the
patient that he needs an urgent back operation, and the flock moves
on. It disperses after the ward round, and its most junior member
returns to write up the young man's chart. She is about to dash to her
next task when the patient calls out, 'Will the operation make me walk
again?' The junior doctor hesitates. 'That's unlikely, but it will stop
things getting worse.' The patient nods and turns his head away. The
junior doctor hesitates again, then leaves as her beeper goes off.

Caring has once again not been provided. How many times could
we instance this in our highly pressured health system? It should, of
course, be a health-*care* system. The distinction is clear, as related by
Professor Ian Graham, the distinguished cardiologist, in a lecture
entitled 'Hurt and Healing' that he gave in 2002:

> Referral letters to the clinic are often simple, reflecting the fact that
> family doctors are under extreme pressure of time to see all their
> patients. For example,
>   'Dear Dr —, Chest pain. Heart? Please advise.'
> Usually one knows within about 20 seconds that the problem is
> environmental and not due to organic disease. Often a simple
> question such as 'Perhaps you would like to tell us what is going on'
> releases the floodgates. Recently, a lady in her 40s, whose pain was

clearly of the spirit and not of the body, said, 'Well, doctor, my children are on drugs, in prison or both; my neighbours are mostly drunk and abusive, and I see no-one I can talk to for days on end. I don't trust the priest and I don't go to mass any more. Last week, my husband walked out. As he slammed the door he said, "And anyway, you're fat".'

To what extent, if any, are the current managerialist policies of the Health Service Executive directed to enabling health-care staff to *care* for people? Providing treatment for physical ailments as cheaply and efficiently as possible is the easy part; providing *caring* requires a revolutionary shift of attitude as to what the whole enterprise of health care is about.

I have for long been an enthusiast and advocate of voluntary health-care organisations—not because I think they are without their faults but because at the heart of what they do is *caring*, in which the best of the human spirit is applied to the resolution of human suffering. The courage of those in Positive Action, the compassion displayed by TRUST, the friendship evidenced by GROW—and these examples could be multiplied literally by hundreds—are priceless aspects of caring social action. Where often the state sees only costly problems, volunteers see opportunities for love and affirmation, regardless of the status or condition of the recipient. Dr Maureen Gaffney has well expressed this:

. . . dependence is part of the human condition. And those who are dependent need care. And care needs intimacy and contact, so that we are alert to the cues that the dependent person is giving us, so that we can respond to their needs.

Dr Leonard Condren has pointed to the danger of being 'pre-occupied with computers, scanners and scopes to the detriment of our focus on the predicament of the sick person.' He wisely advises that doctors concentrate on the 'seminal event,' which is their consultation with the patient. This is built upon trust between the patient and the doctor. This trust has to be earned by the doctor, and that means time and attention given to the relationship. Dr Condren says that the doctor

respects a person by engaging with them, empathising with them and actively listening to them. Active listening is a much more dynamic process than simply hearing what a person says. It means paying attention to the totality of what the person is communicating to you. It also means observing the person's body language as they speak.

Remembering where our true treasure of genuine healing is to be found in health care requires a major refocusing upon the art of healing as much as, or even more than, the science of healing: it means giving the humanities an integral place with the natural sciences at the core of the preparation for, and the practice of, medicine and nursing. I say 'remembering,' because so many great doctors in the past, and indeed some in the present, practise the kind of humane medicine that is in such a general danger of being forgotten. One example is Dr Paul Tournier (1898–1975), perhaps the last century's most famous physician, who practised for nearly fifty years in Geneva what he called 'the medicine of the person' and described it in his many books, such as *The Healing of Persons* (1940). In the twenty-first century, rediscovering this 'treasure' of true healing will mean learning from the field of hospice and palliative care, which has so much to teach every health-care practitioner.

Dr Michael Kearney, consultant in palliative medicine, wisely chose D. H. Lawrence's poem 'Healing' to preface his seminal book *Mortally Wounded: Stories of Soul Pain, Death and Healing* (1996), which ought to be mandatory reading for all who care for others. It provides a fitting statement of what I am trying to convey also.

> I am not a mechanism, an assembly of various
>   sections.
> And it is not because the mechanism is working
>   wrongly, that I am ill.
> I am ill because of wounds to the soul, to the deep
>   emotional self
> and the wounds to the soul take a long, long time,
>   only time can help
> and patience, and a certain difficult repentance,
> long, difficult repentance, realisation of life's
>   mistake, and the freeing oneself
> from the endless repetition of the mistake
> which mankind at large has chosen to sanctify.

Fergus O'Ferrall is director of the Adelaide Hospital Society. He is the author of *Citizenship and Public Service: Voluntary and Statutory Relationships in Irish Healthcare* (2000) and joint editor (with Kenneth Kearon) of *Medical Ethics and the Future of Healthcare* (2000). He is a part-time lecturer in health services management in the Department of Public Health and Primary Care, Trinity College, Dublin. He is also a Board member of the Adelaide and Meath Hospital, Tallaght, Co. Dublin, and a past chairman of the Wheel, a co-ordinating body for community and voluntary organisations.

Rody's time

Pádraig Ó Macháin

Rody O'Neill was a neighbour of mine and was an extraordinary man. A bachelor farmer, he shared a house for years with his brother Bill, who was hard of hearing. Because of this, Rody developed a measured, clear voice that he took with him into the outside world and that gave him a declamatory presence wherever he went. Bill died in 1997, and Rody spent his remaining years alone.

He was a good example of the principle that living alone need not equate with loneliness. He had a circle of friends and neighbours who used to visit or *cuartaigh* with him at night, and he was a great man for returning the compliment. His hurling prowess in his youthful years—he won an all-Ireland junior medal with Kilkenny—made him well known beyond the bounds of the parish of Galmoy, and his active interest in amateur dramatics derived from a personality that had a lot of roguery and no element of shyness in it. He had a great memory for people and events of bygone days and was well able to tell a story or sing a song. To this mixture of characteristics was added a genuine curiosity in his fellow-man, and in the world in general.

Perhaps the most outstanding characteristic of Rody O'Neill, however, was his attitude to time. Depending on one's point of view, it could be exhilarating or exasperating. Rody had time for everyone and anyone. It was not that he *made* time: he just had it. A journey to town on a simple single errand might take all morning, or the best part of the day, depending on what chance encounters occurred. A pressing engagement would lose its urgency if Rody met a neighbour or an old friend or hurling opponent along the way; and what others might consider delay, digression or distraction became for him the central purpose of that day.

I well remember returning with him from a match in south Kilkenny, hurrying back to some now-forgotten appointment at home, when, an idea suddenly occurring to him, his car made an alarming and unannounced swerve. Some minutes later we were standing at an uncharted crossroads, Rody tapping on the door of a low house that anyone else would have thought derelict. A weak voice invited us in, and as we crossed the threshold it seemed that we were stepping into the nineteenth century. It was dark inside, but against the far wall I could make out an iron bed that held the frail body of a man who was now greeting us with a smile. Around him on the wall were hung a Rosary beads and a collection of faded holy pictures. Rody sat on the side of the bed, and the conversation with this old hurling friend and adversary of his went on for hours, while I just marvelled at it all.

New experiences held a particular attraction for him. When I suggested that the two of us head off one night for a singing pub in Co. Tipperary he readily agreed. When we arrived he was an instant hit, making friends with all in his own gregarious way, having a word for everyone and a couple of songs to cement the impression he made on all present. A teetotaller all his life, he delighted in the company to be found in rural public houses, and in adding to his vast stock of knowledge of human nature. (The only time he broke his Pledge was when, at his request, we drank a drop of brandy together a few days before he died.)

It was a characteristic of his that if on a journey of the kind that we had undertaken this night, he would always try to return by a different route from the one he had taken on setting out. Thus it was that, with some alarm, I observed us leaving the pub and heading off at midnight in the opposite direction to the one we had come. An early morning tour of darkest Tipperary ensued before I finally stumbled to my bed at 4:30 a.m.

One summer it happened that I had my turf cut in a particularly inaccessible part of the bog. To get it home after I had saved it would entail packing it all into about three hundred bags and then barrowing the bags out to my car-trailer on the bog road, a conveyance that could take only twenty bags at a time. It was going to be a particularly arduous task, and I was not relishing it.

After filling the bags I thought about the situation for a while before asking Rody if he would oblige me by bringing over his tractor and trailer, which he could drive onto the bog and which could accommodate all the bags of turf in one go. Rody had never saved turf in his life, so this was new and interesting territory for him.

With tractor and trailer he duly arrived on the bog one sunny morning. Like the novice he was, he drove straight onto the spreading ground, where the hind wheels of the tractor immediately proceeded to sink slowly into the soft earth. The more Rody revved the engine and twisted the steering-wheel, the more the tractor became entrapped. To crown the affair, a stone became lodged on the rim of one of the wheels, which, as the wheel spun, swept the valve from the tyre and released the wind with a swift gush into the fresh morning atmosphere.

When Rody finally gave up, the tractor resembled the last moments of the *Titanic*, with its bow practically vertical and its stern hidden in the depths of a black, unfathomable grave. All thoughts of turf were now forgotten as the community of turf-savers gathered from the far ends of the bog to remark upon the situation and to offer solutions to our worrying predicament. Worrying, that is, for everyone except Rody. For him it was a God-sent opportunity to meet people he had not seen for half a century, to renew acquaintances and to make new ones among the progeny of those against whom he had hurled many decades before.

While I sat embarrassed on a bog-bank wondering where the helicopter could be found that would wrench the tractor from the hungry grasp of the bog, Rody was off tracing relationships and genealogies—a particular talent of his—with all the onlookers. Indeed it appeared to me that to have raised the tractor any time before dusk would have been an inconvenience, and practically an impertinence, to Rody, for whom, in his particular scheme of things, farming and farm machinery were only sad distractions from the vital business of communicating with his fellow-man.

After a struggle of nearly ten hours, with the help of another tractor, a strong chain, many timber planks and sheets of corrugated iron, we eventually drew Rody's tractor out of the bog-hole and had the stricken wheel taken away for repair. The shy slither of a new moon was rising as I walked along the earthen track, trying to find my neighbour. I heard his voice as it travelled clearly over the surface of the heather, and at last I spotted him in the distance, deep in conversation with a man as old as himself. Both were oblivious of the hour of day, of the gathering dark, and of the exigencies of humanity at large. They were using their time in the way that the God who made it and who gave it to them had intended it to be used. The rest of us, covered head to foot in damp black earth, had fretted and worried for many hours about something that in Rody's scheme was without importance. The turf was destined to go up in smoke, and the tractor was simply another possession that no coffin would accommodate.

Pádraig Ó Macháin is a professor in the Dublin Institute for Advanced Studies. He lives on a smallholding in Co. Kilkenny with his wife, Joan, and their six children.

Living life

Chinedu Onyejelem

There is an old saying that life begins at forty. For those who believe in that it is a source of encouragement and energy to keep up the struggle in life, with the hope that by the time they turn forty, things will basically change for them—perhaps overnight?

Others would disagree with this sentiment. One day I had an opportunity to discuss this with a controversial friend of mine who has an opinion on almost everything on earth. According to him, if life begins at forty it means that the first forty years of life have already been lost. His attitude is 'Make the most of life, and don't wait till you are forty.'

Indeed, I agree with him on that. Many people who are looking forward to enjoying themselves when they turn forty seem to be envisaging a false paradise. Sceptics would strongly argue that the 'life begins at forty' maxim should not be taken too literally.

A parallel would be the story of Jesus feeding thousands with very, very little fish and loaves of bread; the same sceptics would say it was a fiction designed to instil moral and responsible living in human beings. Nevertheless, those who believe in that are still entitled to do so, even if they are hoping against hope.

Whatever you think yourself, the point is that to live well—I mean to enjoy life, whether at ten years of age or at forty—you need to have some sort of a game plan. One needs to know exactly what one is looking for in life.

I have come across people who think that their misfortune—their inability to measure up to certain expectations in life—was because the Celtic Tiger was not evenly distributed to everyone in the country. Some others, especially our new African immigrants, tend to believe that some sort of gods have destined them to eternal failure. Sometimes it is just their mind-set that is preventing them from taking great strides towards solving their personal problems and therefore becoming the person they want to be.

Indeed, the unfortunate thing about the state of one's mind is that it becomes a target for abuse. I have seen how sometimes religion—for example some born-again churches and some Islamic sects—has become manipulative to those it is meant to lead and thereby destroys the human values that make up people and society. Many people seem to be suffering from mental colonialism through them.

What a waste of people's life! Life should be about living—about freedom from a myopic mind-set and forced and false thinking. We are in a century where globalisation means much more than nations and their interaction with others. It is a world where new ways of living and mental freedom should prevail.

Living life should be an everyday thing.

Chinedu Onyejelem, editor and publisher of *Metro Éireann,* Ireland's only multicultural newspaper, is a winner of the ESB-Rehab People of the Year award (2006). He founded the Metro Éireann Media and Multicultural Awards and the Permanent-TSB Ethnic Entrepreneur of the Year award. He is a ministerial nominee to the Steering Group of the National Action Plan Against Racism and a member of the Department of Foreign Affairs NGO Standing Committee, which advises the Government on human rights issues overseas. He was recently appointed a non-executive director of Concern Worldwide.

Unseen Outsiders

Catherine Pearson

I write for the Unseen Outsiders. They are not to be found living on the streets of Ireland's cities or villages but within their homes. They have had no children, or their once-young families are scattered. They are proud, they feel useless, they do not wish to be pitied, they are alone—they are old!

They can be seen, dressed neatly, on public transport, shop-gazing or in the supermarkets. Their income is small; they 'manage.' They are not easy to find, or to contact. They do not ask for anything to be *done* for them. They would appreciate *sharing* an event.

Do not be upset by rejection. Find them, and enjoy wasting time *with* them.

Catherine Pearson, a 'people person,' is a member of the Religious Society of Friends (Quakers) and a member of the Irish Society of Chartered Physiotherapists.

Listening can ease the journey

Patrick Plunkett

I work in a busy emergency department. Most people attend here only once, or perhaps once every five years. Everybody wants to be seen immediately, yet most will wait for hours to be seen. How can I justify wasting any time? But each person who crosses the threshold has their own story, their own failings in life, their thwarted ambition, their grief and sadness. It is possible that you will never experience such sadness yourself, though unlikely that even you will escape from life's tragedies. If you have not experienced such sadness, remain hopeful.

Recently I saw a middle-aged man walking down the middle of the corridor, then leaning against a wall in an area supposedly closed to the public. As I saw him I was about to ask, 'Can I help you?'—a euphemism for 'Why are you somewhere you shouldn't be?' But I realised that he was struggling to breathe and leaning against the wall in order not to fall.

Tommy, for that is the name I will give him, had such a severe attack of asthma that he had to be admitted to hospital, following emergency treatment that enabled him to breathe and to speak. As I started to treat him the receptionist came to obtain his details for registration. She was taken aback when he declared that he had no fixed abode. NFA—this clean-shaven, well-dressed, polite man? Surely there must have been some mistake. Our regular NFA types are dirty, smelly, with torn, soiled clothing and at least a few days' stubble as a general rule. And no mobile phone? For the receptionist this was a bridge too far. How could we communicate with him later if he had no address and no phone? No next of kin was the last straw for her. Surely he had to have someone! As it turned out, his mother lived in a provincial town, but he had no contact with her.

I had to remain close to him over the next while, during his therapy, given how sick he was. I was allowed into his secrets bit by bit. He had lived abroad and had been married for two years. The marriage had, in his own words, lasted two years too long. It had been a mistake from the beginning, but that was a long time ago. His only regret was that he had no contact with his now-teenage daughter. He had started drifting but, unlike so many others, had not found any need to immerse himself in alcohol to survive the cold of the streets at night. No; he was a businessman of sorts. He went out with a bucket, rag and ladder and cleaned windows for a living. Cash in hand, he had no need for bank guarantees, the paperwork of taxation, reports to shareholders, or costly overheads for a fancy office. Once he had earned enough he would book in to a cheap bed-and-breakfast or a hostel for a few nights, stashing his business equipment in a hidey-hole. He lived frugally. If you don't buy fags or booze, your money lasts much longer.

Was he happy? Well, most of the time. Except when he thought of his inability to see his daughter. That pained him greatly. But he had the freedom of deciding when and where to work, and to lay his head at night. That was priceless for him.

In a sense, he reminded me vaguely of the Needleman. When I was growing up in Ballyfermot, a suburb very much smaller then than now, he would call to the house every three or four months. His title came from the fact that he would sell cards of sewing needles to his customers. He told me once that he was originally a Waterford man. He walked everywhere, sleeping rough beneath a hedge. In those days there were many open fields and hedgerows between Ballyfermot and the railway line, with the adjacent Grand Canal. We knew the area as the 'Backers'. He had a billycan and a bundle of blankets, which he would hide beneath a hedge before doing his rounds.

He was careful to make it clear that he was not a beggar: he was a salesman with a product. If one wished to pay more for his needles than one would in the city centre, he was happy to provide the door-to-door convenience. He was grateful for a cup of tea and a sandwich but would only eat them on the doorstep; he resolutely declined to enter the house. If asked whether there was anything else he could do with, his reply was always the same: some tea, or some sugar, in a twist of paper, and, if it wasn't too much trouble, a scrap of soap, so he could wash and shave.

Over the years he gradually became more stooped and more feeble of voice, while his pace slowed. His lower eyelids began to droop outwards, giving him a rheumy, bloodshot appearance. This condition, known as ectropion, is easily treated surgically, but he was not in a position to seek such assistance. Indeed when it was mentioned to him he simply shrugged his shoulders and said it never really bothered him.

As the years passed, the houses began to extend southwards, closing off his old habitat. One year, he didn't appear. I never saw him again but hope and trust that he found a peaceful place to rest his weary bones.

Jimmy and Johnny are two regulars in the emergency department. They frequent whichever emergency department the ambulance brings them to, whenever they have drifted over the boundary into a neighbouring area before lying down under the weight of drink and waiting for some kind person to call the Big White Taxi—for such is the function of the ambulance service for those who are so incapable of self-care as to be at risk of death from exposure.

As they recover from the stupor brought on by cheap cider or the occasional treat of some weak vodka they become truculent and, if disturbed, aggressive. Their need is to spend some hours in a dry, warm place. They rarely get the opportunity to explain themselves, as they are treated like pariahs by most. They stink, because they wet their trousers and have no means to wash them. At times their clothes are destroyed and they get the benefit of some donated clothes from the stash kept by the social worker.

They usually lurch out of the waiting-room at daybreak, unless it is raining heavily, because they must get some alcohol again before they are visited by the demons of withdrawal. Acute withdrawal from alcohol in someone who is dependent on it is a painful process. They get jittery, and then shake uncontrollably. They may vomit and, if unlucky, will have an epileptic seizure. Unlucky, I say, but there is a hidden benefit in a seizure. As it is so dramatic, they are likely to be brought back in the Big White Taxi.

It is potentially lethal to have alcohol withdrawal seizures (or 'rum fits', as they were known in a previous century), so they will end up as in-patients for a few days, be given drugs to sedate them, and filled with vitamins and calories. It is at such times that they may begin to speak of some of the horrors they experience. But they generally keep such matters quiet, for they know they will not be believed.

To be included in their confessions is a privilege of sorts. But it is also a burden, for the inhumanity suffered by these men (and a few women) at the hands of others is too much to remember. They describe being beaten simply for the sake of being beaten, or being rolled over and their few possessions rifled from urine-sodden pockets, even being sexually abused at times.

'Why do you drink like this?' I ask.

'Because I have to. I sleep rough. It's cold and often wet. I can't sleep without drink to numb the senses. Then I get so cold I can't move, even if someone tries to hurt me.'

What I find so sad is that these men are so much more pleasant and human-appearing after a few days' rest, recuperation and replenishment in a warm bed. But then it all begins again.

The hardest part of my life is telling a person that their loved one has died. Sometimes this is an expected outcome and a relief for all concerned. It is still sad, as the person I am addressing will no longer have any response from the person they are speaking to. And they do speak to them, in a quiet room, often apologising for shortcomings, or promising to carry out previously agreed matters.

But more commonly, in my setting, death arrives unexpectedly, often in circumstances where plans for the future are disrupted, leaving a void and a concern about what will happen next. At times the death is due to injury, and the bereaved person has the additional psychological pain of contemplating the last moments of their loved one, and whether they have suffered physical pain to an inordinate degree.

I remember three elderly sisters coming to the emergency department, with the youngest of them in extremis—obviously dying. They lived together and looked out for one another. Simple lives for simple people—such was their educational and intellectual status. They were barely capable of shopping, cooking and cleaning for one another; yet they had lived together for eight decades, six of those as independent women. The dying lady had a very advanced breast cancer, indeed the most advanced and dreadful I had ever seen in my professional life. The sisters had simply accepted that she had banged her chest and it had not got any better, despite them putting Savlon cream and cotton wool on it for months.

I was present as she slipped away into what I trust is a better place. But the problem remained as to how to answer the question from her older sister—'What shall we do now, without her?' I could not provide any sensible response.

Six months later I was knocked back on my heels when I recognised the two remaining sisters in a cubicle. The middle one now had locally advanced breast cancer! Despite my open discussion at the previous visit, she had simply ignored her lump. I had to ask the eldest whether she herself had any lumps but got a clear negative. Yet, was it true? How intrusive in people's lives can one reasonably be? Would it ultimately make any difference to her?

One dread in my professional life, and yet one of the most important moments, is when I see tears well up in the eyes of the person I am with. Such tears are the outpourings of the soul. Once they start to develop, the astute professional has a few seconds to divert attention, make a break and move the consultation on. In that way, the timetable can be adhered to, and the patient can be let out the door with the mutual expression of satisfaction, however hollow it may be. But to allow the tears to flow can be cathartic for the patient. It needs an effort from the doctor to allow the time, for there are often others outside who are keen to be seen and get away.

I took a phone call from a woman a few weeks ago. She had made strenuous efforts to find me—not as difficult as all that, I thought, given that I haven't moved my office or work space more than fifty metres in twenty years. She had a major illness, of a chronic nature, needing specialist care, but wanted to speak to me, as she needed reassurance and help in obtaining such care. But why call me? Her name meant nothing to me.

She carefully explained how, more than ten years previously, I had made her original diagnosis when she had come in as an emergency. So what? That's my job, but then I hand over to another doctor for long-term care. Her memory was that there had been a resistance to specialised investigation at the time and that I had 'fought' for it to be provided to her. This had eventually proved my initial working diagnosis, potentially saving her life but committing her to lifelong treatment. She had since moved down the country, was having difficulty being believed about her recurring symptoms, and wanted me to sort her out.

It was a difficult situation for me professionally; resolution was possible with a few phone calls and a 'Yes' response from others. It is the 'Yes' attitude that epitomises the colleagues I work with and that is an enormous enablement in my professional life.

This episode reminded me of just how much importance people attach to being listened to.

Despite the increase in communication skills courses for professionals, there is still a dearth of time for communication. Communication must be in both directions. For a doctor to speak before listening is to short-circuit the communication, and to blight it. The relationship between patient and doctor (or master and servant, for such is the real relationship, in my view) is very time-dependent. Too much time spent with one patient leaves too little time for the next. But each has a story. All will die some day, but the journey through life is fraught with hazard and pain. Listening can ease it, for in listening one provides the speaker with the relief of being heard. By taking on part of another's pain one can even become relieved of one's own sufferings.

To paraphrase Martin Luther King during his sermon at Ebenezer Baptist Church, Atlanta, on 4 February 1968, 'If I can help somebody as I pass along . . . then my living shall not be in vain.'

Patrick K. Plunkett is consultant in emergency medicine at St James's Hospital, Dublin, senior lecturer in emergency medicine at Trinity College, Dublin, and editor of the *European Journal of Emergency Medicine*. A colleague once described him as 'a self-aggrandising bastard.' He prefers to be known as one who cares.

Croissants on the Green

Father Brian Power

Croissants on the Green
A coffee shop on Sandymount Green
became a refuge, embodied a dream
of a haven that a soul might seek
when weary and in need of peace.
The menu was adventurous
but it was the welcome surge
that warmed the customer in search
of respite from a world of fuss
and thoughtless incivility.

Pondering
Widowed young, she prayed at the grotto
and pondered the enormity of her loss.
From her height the Madonna consoled
even as she drew the supplicant
into the circle of redeeming pain.
From childhood, the woman thought, I felt
born to suffer, yet can salvage joy
from moments like watching this gull
glide gracefully down the rockface.
Let me be glad I knew the gleam of love
before being drawn to the stony caverns
the Maiden chooses as venues to meet
those who seek acceptance of the divine
and strength to battle till all is changed.

Father Brian Power, born in Dublin in 1930, is a retired diocesan priest. He has written many articles, stories, reviews and sociological reports. Between 1996 and 2006 four collections of his poems were published, and in 1973 he received a Hennessy Award for short-story writing.

Postcard from *Mir*

Suzanne Power

I don't know when I first realised I wasn't going to make it as an insider, but I live with the reality of being an outsider each day.

The weight of my choice and my condition bears down upon me.

Writing, as I am now, from depression, it's not the first time that I've been swallowed. It won't be the last.

For a quarter of a century now I have made my living as a writer, and expect each day to find that living has come to an end. No matter how many column-inches of newspaper or pages of books I fill, I am never good enough for myself. I feel fraudulent.

Dorothy Rowe wrote this wonderful sentence: 'Friendship is our greatest invention.' Wasting time with people is building time with friends, making friends. Modern life leaves little room for friendship. I answer e-mail and make phone calls, but I cannot make enough time to see those that I love. Those who might help me out of the dark room. Those who persuade me I am not a fraud.

Those who TRUST works with, and those who TRUST's work supports, are one and the same. We are all people. We are all struggling. Some of us in the dark room, some of us not. But everyone, no matter how positive, enters the dark room at some stage, whether it be through tragedy or crisis, or both. Very few get through without failing to come to terms with something at some point.

The world hurts. Last night my sons and I looked at the full risen moon through binoculars and I wished I could move there. Being an outsider, whether it happened through nature or through nurture, I am removed from the main frame, and there are days when I do not even want to be part of the edges. Therefore I isolate myself. We all need that sometimes, but the question is, how much?

Albert Camus wrote: 'If we are to understand the world, we must turn aside from it; if we are to serve men better, we must briefly hold them at a distance.'

In a world where everyone can be reached in an instant there is no retreat. We bring satellite telephones to the top of Everest; we send postcards from *Mir*.

We are testing and tasting too much and we are losing our pioneer spirit, because we have no physical boundaries left and no mystery to embrace. To pioneer means to go where others have not gone. Not just physically, but mentally and spiritually.

For this planet, at this time, it is, in my opinion, time to stop. Time to take time. We claim that we are in better health and living longer than any other generation. But we live in a corner of the world that looks at itself in a fairground mirror—the skinny one—and seeks to have all we did not have.

Some call this famine 'consciousness'. The shortage is no longer food. The shortage is not even time. The shortage is in recognising what it means to be truly, fully human. Recognition is what human beings in this tiny, privileged corner of a vast world with concerns that are far more life and death than ours, pile on top of each other for.

But we are looking in the wrong mirrors.

All my life I have been looking for recognition, a reflection in a mirror that has been blackened. I don't mean social recognition, I mean recognition from myself. I wish I could find a way of loving the person that I am, since I am surrounded by love and since I have received a lot in the way of appreciation.

But I drive myself relentlessly, I find reasons to keep myself in a harness, pulling loads that defeat. Since I was a teenager I have been looking for the street, but I am too afraid to end up there. I lack the courage to lose myself entirely, to let go. Some would say this is strength. No. I know it's fear.

The dark room has one bed with a single blanket that is never warm enough. It is always cold. There is no God here, there is just waiting, for something that feels like Godot. One who will never come. It is the nightmare of the existentialist, and I live in it, as someone who carries the thin cords of faith and sustenance. I see how I inspire others in my teaching and in my words and I worry that I am lying. Because I am advising, all the time, people to go after their dreams. To hope.

I look at the people on the street and I know that they are living in a dark place. But somehow, when I speak to people on the street, look into their eyes, I can see that some of them have gone where I am afraid to go. They have the relief of having lost everything. I am in the harness.

I am two people. And for these present days, the dark one is winning. She has had more of my head and heart than the light one. Yes, the reason is the twenty-first century and the relentless nature of living and doing. But it is also this: I see the world as I wish to see it. I fail where others, who have far less than me in material terms, succeed. I empty my own glass.

Since I began writing, my son has been into the room twice— once with a red crepe paper present containing a stuffed toy and once to take a digital photograph of me. He's taken a picture of me as I am. Writing in my dark room, waiting for light. In the past few months I have lost the ability to hope for myself. All my hopes are for him and his brother.

Yesterday I saw a kingfisher on the river bank, and the beauty of it nearly destroyed me. I thought it was a waste to offer such a sight to one such as me. It was a sight better served on my sons, who have brighter hearts and possibilities than mine. And far greater appreciation.

My dark room is one I built myself. How? I drove myself on when I should have rested. I took my healthy body—physical and mental— and replaced it with a goal-oriented creature of deep insecurities. Now that creature has gone, I am left with the question of who I am.

The retreat Camus recommended, the summer, is completely mine. I live a life where I can reach the city only by phone. I hear bird-song first thing and see bats winging last thing at night. I know the seasons. It makes it all the more painful to live with the unmanageable feelings. My mind is a bomb site.

It comes down to one thing. I have never had enough courage to rest, unless I was forced to by illness. I have not had sufficient faith to wait and to trust.

Wasting time. It's the time we think we are wasting that is so important. Children, the children who keep me in the world, have taught me that. All the idleness of being is what we are missing now. When we plan outings and holidays we are inviting idleness. But we are also standing in ragged airport queues, with overwhelming amounts of luggage, catching planes to places far away, to feel what we could feel at home.

Last week I was with a lot of children, giving them my enthusiasm for books and for living with the right to dream. If you have the confidence to be the person you were made to be, then you don't lose your dreams. You cope. You take knocks. The children began the week as wonderful and ended up being more than wonderful. They were like stars in a constellation, shining bright and determined and fierce in their self-belief. I observed them in my space station. More than one of them, in quiet moments, came to share their condition with me.

I am lucky to suffer with great sensitivity and to be someone who lives with depression. I am lucky that I am someone who walks the tightrope between making it and not making it. Because when I am well I am very well. And I can see with eyes that others, who are more level in their living style and circumstances, maybe have lost. I can spare breath and time and eyes and ears for those who need help, no matter what state I am in.

I cannot walk past those who have lost everything. I am so close to losing it myself. The street people are my brothers and sisters.

The letter that came with the request to contribute to this book asked some questions. What can we do? The answer is nothing. Nothing is an action. You wait until the right moment comes along and then the opportunity presents itself to make a change, a difference.

You wait. Waiting is an action. I was taught that by nature and the heron's place in it, fishing for itself, studying its reflection for hours, before moving, at speed, when the right time comes to feed.

This postcard is from *Mir*. My space station. The place of retreat I have created out of a desire for solitude and an inability to deal with people.

I trust one day that I will feel better and return not only to people but to myself. A person who I don't know yet.

Whether you have a faith in the eternal, or a faith in humanity, you must have faith in yourself. It is a requirement of the human race that we do not rob ourselves of that. And that we, at every opportunity, offer it to those we come across. Because in doing so we are offering it to ourselves.

Suzanne Power has been writing since she was eight, and her short stories and travel writing have featured in anthologies. She is also a columnist with the *Evening Herald*. The rights of her first three novels—*Lost Souls' Reunion, The Virgo Club* and *Love and the Monroes*—have been sold around the world and she is finishing a fourth. Together with John MacKenna she has set up a creative writing course through the National University of Ireland's adult education centre in Kilkenny.

I'll get back to you

Terry Prone

My husband put down the phone, shaking his head and smiling. 'Anton and you play variations on the same signature tune,' he observed. 'He always says, "Ring you back in five minutes." You always promise to be back in three.'

In reality, I tend to make the promised call within about an hour, if the wind is in the right direction. Our son's five minutes? Could be a day later. A week later. Never.

It's not that he doesn't want to; he adores his father. It's that someone else lands in his in box or text screen or phone, or pitches up in person in front of him, or he has a meeting or will have his car clamped. It's not like he's sittin' on the dock of the bay, wastin' time, like that old song.

None of us are. We're busy. Omigod, we're so *busy*.

Mostly, we're busy with the care and feeding of the gadgets that were supposed to hand us back our lives and put us into the leisure classes. E-mail, for instance. Great invention. Except for the people who send jokes. It's a little-known fact of nature that no joke circulated on the internet was ever worth sending, but I have friends who have a joke habit. If they don't send a joke a day to all their friends they get the bends. Early on, when I bitched about this, a pal suggested that at least joke circulation gave you access to the e-mail addresses of all the people to whom the joke-senders were transmitting their daily giggle. I bought in to this for about a week. Then I found that joke-senders have the kind of friends you'd only want the e-mail address of if you were another joke-sender, and being in there with them frazzled my sense of self-worth.

Not that my feelings of self-worth were that high anyway, because of the spam. Everybody gets it. Unless my female friends are lying to

me, though, not many of them get six offers per day of penis enlarge-
ment, the way I do. Who are these people who think I need not just a
whatsit but a *bigger* whatsit? How did they pick me? How can I get
them to unpick me?

By the time the jokes and penises are deleted, it's down to finding
what messages actually matter in the remainder. Some of them, merci-
fully, are terse responses to messages I sent the day before, with my
message hanging there to remind me. My sister confuses the hell out of
me by sending enigmatic responses to messages I've forgotten, without
appending them. 'That might be appropriate,' her e-mail will say. 'But
what about tax law and the archbishop?' I have to go back to my sent
messages to establish that she hasn't mislaid her final marble.

And then there are the messages that come with little red flags
attached. The sender of this message requires an instant response.
Well, to hell with that sender.

My mobile phone (okay, let's name-drop: it's a Blackberry) has
three different squawks: one for phone calls, one for text, and one for
e-mail. I could turn it to mute and let it just vibrate, but somehow a
vibration is more exigent than a squawk, not least because my animal
brain overrides reality for a crucial few seconds, convincing me I'm
touching a live wire.

Time management courses can blither for ever about learning
not to sacrifice the Important to the Urgent, but they're wasting
their breath. Our addiction to the immediate is impregnable. Other
addictions are so clearly counter-productive that people end up in
Alcoholics Anonymous or Narcotics Anonymous or Gamblers
Anonymous, but addiction to the immediate is validated as part of
productivity, part of being a good parent. You have to be *available*.
If you're not running late for every meeting, or fail to get six text
messages during lunch, then you can't be doing that well, you
mustn't be that important.

When you get home in the evening you're so stressed out from all
this busy-ness that you have to slump in front of the television,
the Monster That Ate Up Time. I know, I know. You only watch the
news and the current affairs programmes to keep up to date. None of
us know the morons who watch all the other programmes while
simultaneously recording 'The Apprentice' so they can view it later.

We have to do this stuff now, but we'll get around to the other
stuff. It's just this particular month, you know? *Chronically* busy. And

with the baby, between sterilising the bottles and mixing the feed and varying the tunes on the Playbox in the cot, things have just gone crazy. But we'll get back to you.

In fact, if anybody had the time those Gospels need a rewrite to bring them up to date. That Good Samaritan, for example. You wouldn't have to change his character. He would still have nothing but the best intentions towards the guy who got mugged. If he spotted him in the gutter, which he might not—you know yourself when you're trying to walk and text at the same time—if he saw the guy, though, he'd make an immediate generous promise. 'I'll get back to you.'

Terry Prone is a writer, broadcaster and communications expert. She is married to Tom Savage, and their son is Anton.

Children first and always

Sister Fiona Pryle

When I think back on when I returned to Ireland twenty-two years ago, everything about life is very different. The speed, the volume of traffic—there is a huge change in the pace of life. There have always been challenges. They are just different challenges now, and I feel that life is extremely stressful for people. The divide between the 'haves' and the 'have-nots' has become much more marked.

As I awake every morning my guiding principle is that I am an agent to go out and do anything within my capabilities to make sure that people live their lives to the full. It means constantly journeying with them, and challenging the unjust structures that surround children first and also women in domestic violence situations—two of the most vulnerable groups in our society today. For the most part, however, my motto is 'Children first, last, and always.'

A sentence in John's Gospel, 'I came that you may have life—life to the full,' is my guiding principle in how I interact with people and how I view life. As far as is possible I try not to let the surrounding pressures affect my work. I don't care what is going on around me. When I am with a person they have my undivided attention. I can offer this because I consider that I have been fortified through the very full life that I enjoy, and I want to see others having what I have.

There has been widespread reporting about the huge differences in our society, and how the boats have not lifted for a lot of people. This is in spite of the economic boom that Ireland has experienced in the last ten years. I find myself questioning the value system that has evolved around this 'boom' and see how much of this is contrary to the wellbeing of the nation's children. Many people still have not made the link between child welfare, their rights and the future they will occupy in our society.

I can remember being with a businessman and asking for his support towards funding for the Children First Foundation. I did my best to explain to him the motto of our congregation's foundress, St Mary Euphrasia: 'A person is of more value than a whole world.' This was the legacy of investing in children. He replied very vigorously, 'That doesn't make any sense.' I said, 'Well, it makes sense to me.'

I found his response disturbing and incomprehensible. How could I convey to a group of business people that each child is truly precious? By offering children hope through the medium of music, dance and sport, for example, you create a whole new way of life. You pull them back from the social and economic 'black hole' that surely awaits them. Not only that, by intervening at this level you create a whole new world view in a family. Yet still this man thought this message complete and utter nonsense.

Anyone who knows me knows that who and what I stand for is more often than not contrary to what people's world view is. Gordon Brown said in his inaugural speech, 'There isn't so much a poverty of income as the poverty of aspiration.' This echoes my sentiments about aspiration and hope. Where these ingredients are introduced and nurtured in a family, at whatever stage, it is equivalent to offering them an escalator to the next floor—an invitation into a brighter, wider, better world view.

When children are raised in poverty it is a fact that this places them at high risk for a wide range of problems, risk factors that can result in impaired brain development and affect social and emotional development. Very often these children will have been exposed to poor nutrition, parental substance abuse, maternal depression, parental conflict, trauma, violence or divorce from early infancy. This pattern paves the way for poor health, learning difficulties, increased aggression, delinquent behaviour and mental health problems from adolescence onwards and into a very bleak future.

There is not enough investment in children, and children are not centre stage as they should be. We see and hear about this in our Constitution and how efforts are being made to move them to centre stage. Can anyone tell me for certain when this is going to happen?

The Government are re-elected now and are full of promises to all sections of the community. The reality for children in deprived areas of our country, born into families where parents have no aspirations, for different reasons, means that they can have no aspirations. This is a lethal ingredient for their future, and for the future of Ireland.

The Government needs to direct a significant investment into pre-schooling, which can be provided for children at a very early age, provide extracurricular activities in school and provide early intervention in these families. The focus and investment need to be into these communities, and less into Mountjoy. This is the best route to emptying our prisons.

My fervent desire is to persuade businesses to invest in a child and a family in order to change their world view; to offer them an opportunity to come fully into life. It's lovely to see children from poorer areas that are part of a society that has formerly excluded them blossom, simply because a path has been created for them to be part of a dance group and opening up an opportunity for them to compete and win medals etc.

Through our work we can put them into the mainstream of life that excludes them because they live in deprived areas. It also provides opportunities for holidays for children who would never be able to come out of their environment. Our goal is to address businesses and encourage them to commit themselves to the life-cycle of a child to young adulthood, and see that child graduate eventually to some meaningful career choice.

Through corporate social responsibility, agencies can bridge the gap between the 'haves' and the 'have-nots'. This is my challenge to the world of business.

We can all work together to help our children and ensure that their time in this world is quality time. For all our sakes.

A sample case history of our work: One child began with a single parent in Tallaght, Co. Dublin. We'll call him James. His father was in prison. We came across the boy, aged twelve, by contacts with the hostel for homeless boys with which I worked in Percy Place and Eccles Street from 1985 to 1994.

James's father had been in care, as had his father before him. James was third generation and being kept at home, just surviving. His mother was barely coping, and his father was in and out of the drug scene. James was a very bright child and he had the motivation to see what was destructive in his family. He wanted to be different and he was supported by us to be part of the local soccer team and GAA. He was a fantastic kick-boxer and was supported in doing this. He managed to complete secondary school and did well and got a good Leaving Certificate. He did a fitness training management course and is now fully qualified and employed, and talking about buying a house and moving out of the deprived area of his childhood.

This is only one example of how life-altering support can be. James has been an inspiration to his brother and sister, who are also getting our support. The ripple effect on this one child, his family, his friends, colleagues, students—right out into society and the future—has been truly profound.

Sister Fiona Pryle is a native of Co. Meath and a member of the Good Shepherd Congregation. In 1964 she went to England, where she worked in residential care for girls in London, Bath and Manchester. In 1983, after training as a social worker and teacher, she worked in Slough for two years. On returning to Dublin she set up hostels for homeless boys in Percy Place and Eccles Street, where she remained until 1994. She then set up the education and training programme for the Ruhama project before moving to the ASCEND women's project in Co. Tipperary for victims of domestic violence. She works as mentor and co-ordinator of the Children First Foundation in Dublin. She played a special role in the CND peace movement for the Social Justice Network in England and, in Peace '93, the peace movement in Ireland. She is at present involved in the Social Justice Network and local APT (Act to Prevent Trafficking of Persons) movements. She describes herself as having a healthy interest in sports, and loves music and reading.

Goodwill

Feargal Quinn

One of the first things I learnt in my career as a grocer was that shopping is about a lot more than just buying goods for yourself or your family. For many people, shopping is also a very important social interaction with other human beings—whether they are other shoppers or the people who serve them in the shop.

From the beginning, I found myself conflicted: on the one hand, I wanted to bring to Ireland the full benefits of self-service shopping; on the other hand, I wanted to preserve as much as I could of the human benefits of shopping as a social experience.

This is why, as our competitors strove to reduce the number of people working in their shops, I took the opposite approach. I believed I could justify in business terms the use of more people, because I felt that the greater business they created would outpace the extra expense of employing them. Instead of seeing technology as a way of getting rid of people, I saw it rather as a way of increasing the reach of the people we had—helping them to do more in the way of providing a personal service to each of our customers.

Instinctively, people prefer to deal with other people than with machines: that is the natural way of things. The nature of our lives today creates a situation more and more where it is cheaper to have a machine do the simpler tasks. The conundrum is that while it is easy to have a machine deliver to you the cash you need, it is not so easy to get the machine to offer a human greeting or ask how your children are.

In our business we took the risky but very carefully considered step of building what we offered around people, and trying to support them with technology rather than replacing them with it. Over the years I had many fights with accountants, who simply couldn't see the bottom-line value of having customers who were more pleased to have a few words with a friendly butcher than to select the meat they wanted from a refrigerated display of pre-packed items.

It was a constant struggle that became more difficult as time went on. But I remain convinced today as much as I ever was that business eliminates the personal, human touch at its peril. It is not only the customers who benefit from my approach: business benefits as well, since people will tend to vote with their feet to enjoy the human interaction if they have the choice.

I learnt in the grocery business how important it was to take the time to set an example, rather than simply telling people what to do or printing out a long list of rules for them to follow. For me, a prime example of this was in keeping the floor of our shops free of litter. Whenever I was in any of our shops, if I happened to see a piece of stray litter on the floor I would pick it up—no matter what I happened to be doing at the time or who I was talking to. I quickly noticed that others saw what I was doing, and they were encouraged to do likewise. Over a very short period we built up a strong culture of keeping our shops litter-free, with everyone taking part in the same way, no matter what their role in the shop.

Incidentally, I don't restrict my obsession about picking up litter to my own premises: I will do it anywhere! One day I was walking past the Shelbourne Hotel and saw a newspaper on the ground. Everybody walking past was stepping over it and I thought I better just pick it up and put it into the wastepaper bin. But just before I did it a young man ahead of me bent down and picked it up and stuffed it into the litter bin. As I came up to him I said, 'Well done. You beat me to it,' and then I looked at him closely and realised it was young Tony Darcy from our Ballinteer branch.

I was chuffed, because I don't know that he would have done it before he came to work in Superquinn, but it was part of the culture that he learnt when he was with us. He did it naturally, just as I was going to—the power of personal example. Of course leading by example takes a lot longer to do than other ways of laying down the law, and many people would consider it wasted time. But I don't.

Over the years I have been in business, life has certainly become more hectic, and as a result the demands we have had to make on our colleagues have become greater. But I tried never to forget the importance of having people enjoy what they did and get satisfaction from it every day. One year I remember a man called John Davitt came to me in mid-December and told me that he was planning to retire at the end of the month, on his sixty-fifth birthday. He explained that he had worked for Superquinn in Ballinteer for nine years, had not missed a day, and had come to work every day 'looking forward to the day.' He also said that he often looked at his watch thinking it was 4 p.m. to discover it was 6 p.m.—the day seemed to go so fast.

I'm not sure of the different jobs John had during his previous forty or so years of employment, but clearly he had enjoyed those nine years in Superquinn. Sadly, he died on Christmas Day that year, six days before he was due to retire. In addition, his wife died a few days later. I attended two funerals within a few days of each other. At those funerals I was reminded of John's words: 'I looked forward to the day,' and 'I thought it was 4 p.m. when it turned out to be 6 p.m.' That was the day I decided that there was a new challenge for our company: to make it the best place to work in Ireland.

One of the best lessons I ever learnt in the value of 'wasting' time was something that happened to me in America. I went to visit Reader's Digest in White Plains, New York, because we were interested in learning more about direct mail, and Reader's Digest is regarded as one of the biggest direct-mailers in the world. I arrived in La Guardia Airport—my wife, Denise, was with me—and we took the Avis rent-a-car coach over to Avis, and I said to one of the other passengers who was also going to rent a car, 'Excuse me. Is it far to White Plains, and in what direction will I go?'

He then described how you turn left at the third turn to the right and you went over the Triborough and then you take the second turn to the left and you went over something else and then you went under something else, etc. I said, 'Let me get that again,' and when he described it the second time and I was trying to write it down he said, 'I tell you what—I'm going that direction; just follow me.' Our bags took a little bit longer to check in, but he waited at the exit for us. This is a man I had met for no more than three or four minutes, and he was sitting waiting for us. We came to two different tolls and he paid for me at each toll—one was 50 cents and the other 6 cents. As we got near White Plains he pointed us in our direction and drove off in his direction.

I never saw the man again; but the amount of goodwill he created for a stranger to his country was such that I think of it regularly if I happen to be somewhere and realise that there is somebody who could do with a hand or somebody who is a little bit lost. What is rewarding (in one's own mind) is to pay a toll for a total stranger. On the odd occasion coming to a toll booth you see a tourist car behind you. You say to the toll clerk, 'Take for the person behind, and tell him to have a good holiday!' You know he will never get the chance to say thanks, but it is lovely to do something that makes people feel good.

So that stranger in New York who paid my toll may find that the goodwill he created comes back to benefit him some time.

Feargal Quinn is a member of Seanad Éireann and president of Eurocommerce (Brussels), the retail, wholesale and international trade representation to the European Union. He is also president of Superquinn Ltd, the supermarket company he founded in 1960, which now operates twenty-two supermarkets and nine shopping centres. For a decade he was chairman of An Post. He also serves on the board of directors of CIES, the Food Business Forum (Paris), and the Food Marketing Institute (Arlington, Virginia).

Reading Einstein

Gerard Quinn

I am reading Walter Isaacson's biography of Einstein at the moment. It tells how Einstein constructed complicated equations using 'thought pictures'. His most famous one has a man standing on a railway platform observing trains moving at different speeds and in different directions. He uses this 'thought picture' to develop and explain the theory of relativity, whereby time flows differently according to one's position. I like this 'thought picture', because it often seems to me that time has slowed down or speeded up (usually speeded up), depending on where I am in my life.

Why did life speed up for me, and what were its costs? I was a teenager in the mid-1970s and started college in 1976. From then on time speeded up considerably for me—and not always to good advantage. I always knew that I had to work hard and perhaps harder than most. My mother was a part-time poet and had an enormous love of learning, which she passed on to my brothers and me. Though a top student, she had to leave school at fifteen because of poverty. She worked in the Department of Finance and had a reasonably promising career. But she was forced to leave upon marriage, which was the practice then. I remember that when the marriage ban was eliminated in the 1970s she asked for her job back but was given short shrift.

My father had a difficult life. His mother was murdered by the Black and Tans (it may have been the Auxiliaries) when he was about three years old, and I suppose he never fully recovered from this profound loss in his life.

We had a loving family, and I have especially fond memories of working on my uncle Francie's small farm in west Clare, which is where my mother was from. Despite one's image of a 'valley of squinting windows,' I always found great diversity there and a deep and abiding interest in knowledge about the world.

Using Einstein's 'thought picture', I found the the train pass by slowly—just like the old West Clare Railway! But the view was amazing and colourful. People took a real interest in each other. Farmers helped each other out. Folk memories of Parnell and the War of Independence lingered just beneath the surface—which only emphasised the connectedness of both land and people. Pastimes such as late-night card-playing were popular precisely because there were no interruptions, like television, and people spent a lot of time in each other's company. We all had stories of relatives who made it good in America (we didn't see the hardship they had in a different culture). Even then the straws of change were in the wind. I tended to prefer watching Felix the Cat (and his wonderful bag of tricks) to playing cards!

Education was the key to a better life, and we all knew it. I was a child of the long march towards the Celtic Tiger, which really began in the 1970s. I was the kind of lad who would see a library opened for ten hours and I would reckon there was a reason for that. So I would use it—to the full. I think about 20 per cent of students in the late 70s were very, very driven. The rest had a good time, and I often envy them their experiences. But I was driven. The result was that I got two first-class degrees and went on to study for my master's and doctoral degrees at Harvard Law School. The Harvard experience was intensive and exhilarating, and I retain very strong connections to the faculty. That seems impressive. Yet recently I heard a very senior Harvard figure say that it is the C student who makes the world turn round! I think he was—and is—right. And I think the answer has something to do with the fact that high-achievers are not necessarily well grounded and therefore tend to lose the ability to communicate effectively, to connect with others and to bring people along.

That's the interesting thing. The better—and more professional—you get the more you tend to lose the ability to help improve things for others. If you ask me if I got the balance right I would have to say 'no.' And it is a constant effort to make good that gap.

I have been very happily married to Anne Motherway since 1985 and now have three girls (Niamh, 18, Elizabeth, 10, and Madeleine, 8). Anne is an amazing Cork woman who is incredibly anchored and connected with people. There is a lot written about the need for a good work-home balance. I can't argue with the sentiments. But I can't help wondering whether those who advocate this have ever lived a truly—and I mean truly—pressured life. People are ultimately responsible for themselves. Yet not everything is down to choice. It really angers me that home leave is not paid when it comes to fathers, which of course means there is a predictable imbalance between the numbers of men and women who opt for time off to care for a new baby.

This aspect of the Irish (meaning British) social model is quite pernicious in its effects on family life. In looking at the terms of our social co-existence it seems to me to be wrong to make fathers feel guilty for what the market pressures them into. Our social infra-structure simply does not allow for meaningful periods of family engagement, and that really, really has to change for our children's sake. So I think I made some wrong choices. But I also think we, as a society, have not facilitated and encouraged making better choices. My hope for the future is that fathers will not have to do this.

My train was moving too fast in the early 2000s. My mother got very frail at around that time. I would sometimes work a twelve to fourteen-hour day. My brothers and I had to get a place in a nursing home for her. The home was quite good. Yet I could not get off the treadmill. I visited her often and felt angry at myself for not having more time just to share a laugh. We had the same sense of humour. I think I will go to my grave berating myself for this. And yet I had such few options. My eldest daughter was sick, which required frequent (and unpredictable) stays in hospital. She is fine now and thriving. And my work life was too intense at that period. The only consolation I have is that I now do research on independent living, which will hopefully lead to policy changes in the future to enable the elderly as well as persons with disabilities to live as long as possible in their own settings. This is my way of making up. But intellectualising the issue is no substitute for being in her presence.

My train now is not as slow as the West Clare Railway—yet it is not as fast as a TGV. My children and, especially, my wife have blessed my life with so much more than my career. My wife and children recently met my mother's cousin in Chicago, Marge Carlson, who is ninety and who used to campaign for Franklin D. Roosevelt in the 1930s. It meant a lot to me that they could connect through the generations as well as meet the extended family in America (Butzens,

Kennedys, Kellys, Strickers and many, many others). That's precious beyond words or dollars.

I now know my limits and can see—and hopefully avoid—a treadmill coming from miles away. Success in the narrow career sense has had a heavy price, and I don't think I would pay it again if I had my life all over again. I suppose my generation is only now coming to terms with what we have lost by moving from a policy based on community to one based on individualism. I am still an individualist but instinctively recoil against the possessive individualism of Ireland that only heightens social fragmentation. What I have learnt is that success is a well-rounded concept that is not confined to career. I wish I knew that in 1976.

Gerard Quinn is a professor of law at NUI, Galway. He was called to the Bar in 1983 and has a doctorate in juridical science from Harvard University. He is a former director of research at the Law Reform Commission and led the legal research team of the Commission on the Status of Persons with Disabilities. He has worked with the European Commission on human rights issues as well as on the preparation of EU policy instruments in the field of disability rights. He was director of an EU network of disability discrimination lawyers and now jointly directs a larger EU network on discrimination law on all grounds. He is a former first vice-president of the European Committee of Social Rights (Council of Europe). He was a member of the UN working group convened to draft a treaty on the rights of persons with disabilities. He has published widely on economic, social and cultural rights and on the rights of persons with disabilities.

Once upon a time

Annie Ryan

It is a well-known fact that if one wants a job done it is better to ask a busy person. In general, busy people do not appear to be afflicted by the modern phenomenon of 'time poverty', a concept that is best understood as 'the sense that we don't have the time to do the things we want.' In my mother's generation time poverty was unknown. There was, however, plenty of the other kind, particularly the financial kind. Almost everybody spent long hours trying to survive it.

My parents' generation reared large families without washing-machines, ran farms and milked cows without the aid of machinery, managed shops and engaged in trade when computers were unknown. A lot of time was spent by our immediate ancestors in the effort of producing sufficient wealth for survival, and not always succeeding. Their lives, like ours, had twenty-four hours a day, seven days a week, without the labour-saving devices. So what has happened to all that extra time that should be available to us today?

It is true that we all wash a lot more. Some of us take a shower every day, which is hard on the water supply. Undeniably we are much cleaner. Now that washing-machines have been invented and electricity to use them is provided to every household, our clothes are cleaner too. Routine tasks like darning socks have disappeared, as well as the skills required for their execution. What have we done with all that time saved for us by technology? The answer is, of course, that we have filled it up (or others have filled it up for us) with all sorts of new tasks and new things to do.

Take, for instance, the unremitting task of delivering children to school each morning, picking them up again in the afternoon, as often as not by car. When I was a child it was possible for children to walk safely to school every morning, in the company of neighbours' children. It is a long time now since the Mayo TD Paddy Lindsay, long since dead, pointed out to the Dáil the terrible loss that the introduction of school buses would mean to the children. Few realised at the time what he meant when he described what he himself had enjoyed as he trudged his way to school on the empty Mayo roads. He remembered the corncrake's call and had watched the progress of tadpoles to frogs, all the while developing the social skills (so useful to a politician) in the company of his friends.

The deprivation suffered by the children of today, as well as the hardship of their parents, is undoubtedly the fault of the car. It was the proliferation of the car that made it necessary for the parents to deliver their offspring to their school, usually by car. The roads were no longer safe for little groups of children walking to school—even the roads in Co. Mayo. Families have been known to acquire a car for the specific task of taking the children to school.

Once a family acquires a car they are immediately faced with the cost of running it. The solution is obvious. They are now free to take jobs far away from home, or as far as the car will take them. A whole new dynamic is established.

Once upon a time, settlements—villages, towns, cities—grew up at or near places of employment. Houses followed jobs. Shops, schools and other services followed the houses, or rather the people in them. But the car broke that connection. The houses are where the developer wants them. He does not provide schools or shops, and the jobs may be many miles away. Across the countryside the bright new houses lie empty during the day: no comely maidens, no laughter of little children. No help either for family members who live far away.

This whole absurd situation needs to be rejigged, and of course it will be, as soon as a sufficient number of people realise that they have been robbed. If they haven't time they'll have to make time.

Annie Ryan, a native of Co. Kildare, is a retired schoolteacher, best known for her work of championing the rights of people with an intellectual disability. Her first book, *Walls of Silence* (1999), deals with Ireland's policy towards people with a mental disability. Her two later books, *Witnesses: Inside the Easter Rising* (2005) and *Comrades: Inside the War of Independence* (2007), are based on the statements given by participants in the struggle for national independence. She has continued to campaign for the reform of services for people with an intellectual disability, particularly those accommodated in psychiatric hospitals. She was president of the National Association for the Mentally Handicapped of Ireland from 1992 to 1994 and a member of the Commission for the Status of People with Disabilities and in 1998 received the Rose Fitzgerald Kennedy Mother's Award. She was also a member of the Mental Health Commission from 2002 to 2007.

Cat in my flat

Louisa M. Switzer

I now have a lot of time to 'waste' and to think. My home has been for some years now in St Mary's Hospital, Phoenix Park. I am eighty-four years young. I read, write, think and observe things around me. I write letters to my friends and love getting a letter back.

My home for many years was near Collins Barracks. Sadly, I could never visit it as a museum, and neither could I travel the Luas, which I now read about. I miss the cats: I was always a cat-lover, often walking around late at night to feed strays. People who don't like animals are missing out a lot. Time spent with them is never wasted. Thanks to Dr Brendan O'Donnell from Dublin Corporation, I was allowed to keep my cat until his life (the cat's) ended naturally; some people even complained to him that I had a cat in my flat.

A long time ago I was in an unenviable position, as my partner over-drank. A passer-by told Alice that shouting could be heard coming from our flat, so she tapped on the window one day, and Jim agreed to let her in. She took in the situation and invited me to go to TRUST every morning, and gradually things improved, and Jim would have the dinner ready when I came home. Drink is such a curse, particularly whiskey at a pint a time!

It's so true that if you have no close friends you feel shut out, no-one to share things with. Although I wasn't homeless then, I was prior to getting the flat. We were both homeless for four years. I didn't drink myself, thank God.

When Jim died I missed him so much, even though life was hard at times. I could have just locked myself away from people with only my cat for company. Only for TRUST: they helped me get out and about again, go to the theatre, go on bus tours, eat out, get a phone and use all my entitlements.

I have seen at first hand the terrible sadness of so many lives who would have died only for TRUST's support. I have never forgotten one or two in particular where TRUST was their only mainstay and friend. One or two I knew were illiterate. They told me one young woman I knew committed suicide. She was working as a prostitute and didn't know the value of money and had nothing in sight; she was lost. I used to do her hair in TRUST and bring her a few cream cakes as a treat for herself and her pals. TRUST found little flats for those who could cope, so they felt that all was not lost. Others would never cope. For the little I did I never thought of not having time and never found it mentioned.

This poem was composed by myself when thinking of people I met, wondering about people they knew, and my own experience thinking of Jim.

A wife's lament
For a homeless immigrant

Are you lonely tonight? Have you booked a bed
for a shelter, a roof over your head?
'Twas the demon Drink that drove you away.
It wrecked your body and wasted your pay.
Oh! Where are you staying today?
You have shoes that leak
And you rarely speak of a prosperous yesterday.

But what of Tomorrow? A few shillings you'll borrow
For the price of somewhere to stay!
I'm all alone, you're welcome Home
So please come back *today*!

Louisa M. Switzer is a long-time special friend of TRUST, now residing in St Mary's Hospital, Phoenix Park, Dublin.

Parallel universe

Ronan Tynan

For those anxious to avoid wasting time with people there is a 'solution'. However, every one of us to a greater or lesser extent has become enmeshed in it as well. The great irony is that many of the components were supposed to give us more time for the really important things, like other people, such as our families and friends. However, now the only people who must be truly happy are those who definitely do not want to waste time with people.

I refer to it as a solution but it has many facets, and they all tend to be promoted individually in advertisements as a 'solution'. However, its greatest triumph—or terrifying achievement, depending on your point of view—is that it is now possible for people to live and work as a recluse without any real personal human contact. For example, you can order groceries to be delivered without human contact. You can do your work and earn a living without personal human contact. You can also order such a dramatic and diverse range of things without meeting people or engaging in any human contact at all. In fact you can handle all your personal finances, pay your taxes, all your utility bills—everything, in fact, without even speaking to another human being.

In fact, becoming a hermit or recluse has never been easier, thanks to the myriad of these things that for some reason all tend to be described in marketing literature as a 'solution'. In fact one could earn a living and handle all of life's necessities without stepping outside your front door!

So what is it?

You probably guessed before you finished reading the first sentence.

It is, of course, the myriad of electronic and technological marvels, from the mobile phone to our always-on broadband connection.

But have the liberators become the incarcerators, locking us in to ever more frenetic, always-on lives that have escalated to the point where some of us are even psychologically incapable of turning off our mobiles, and even use them as alarm clocks? These devices and services have given us the ability to communicate in ways undreamt of in the whole history of man; and yet, although it is almost a cliché now that while they have given us a titanic amount of information, and allowed us to deliver to others bizarre amounts as well, have they really brought us closer together as human beings, as distinct from virtual humanoids?

The really frightening thing is how easy it is to completely cut ourselves off, still make a living in a kind of virtual world and never meet real, as distinct from virtual, people. The colourful American billionaire Howard Hughes became even more famous towards the end of his life because he became a recluse, out of a desire to avoid any prospect of wasting time with people, in case he contracted germs or diseases that might prove fatal. Today almost anyone can do it; and no wonder an agency concerned about those whom society appears to have discarded feels it important enough to produce a book to raise the alarm.

All of us must inhabit this virtual world to a greater or lesser degree to make a living and survive. The more we are drawn in, the less time we have, as its appetite to consume us seems to grow exponentially. As we are consumed in this virtual colossus we cannot hear the voices on the margins, because they are not connected. They cannot afford or are unable to be part of this virtual space. The voiceless become even more silent and, worse, even more invisible, if that is possible. We now live in a parallel universe—the virtual and the real; and for some of us, maybe even most of us, the former appears more real than the latter.

Is there a solution?

I have not found one, but at least there is a definite starting point: waste more time with people—off line!

Ronan Tynan is an award-winning documentary filmmaker and joint founder of Esperanza Productions.

Time for the little ones

Bishop Eamonn Walsh

Clutching a bottle in a brown paper bag, wearing a buttonless, stained coat, clean-shaven face on fire, he lunges at me, grabs my arm tightly, sways and says loudly, 'Have you a minute, father?' His request was polite and warm, delivered through missing teeth, with searching, dancing eyes, fired over the years by rejection and self-preservation. He was not requesting money—no, just a prayer and a blessing for a sick friend.

If I had quickened past, as often done before, he would have shouted, muttered and, if near enough, tried to hold me—all very understandable. Often people shout when they experience not being listened to or heeded. Their demand for attention moves up a gear, when they cling on until heard. Initially it can be frightening, but all so understandable once seen as a reaction to regular rejection.

Years of experience sitting on cold granite church entrance steps had shaped Margaret's curved shoulders, drooping head, cupped, weather-beaten outreached hands and her timely upward-pleading glance at passers-by. 'I don't mind the cold, the rain, the long hours or indeed the people who don't give me money,' she said. 'What hurts me to the quick is the person who drops a coin into my hand for fear their hand might touch mine, my flesh contaminate theirs. Are we really the Body of Christ?'

Methadone will keep them ticking over, maintain an equilibrium and keep them away from crime; it's the prefab that becomes the permanent building, an interim measure that can last for life; the drug substitute that can ultimately destroy the vital organs as well as being addictive. Chemical control is less demanding on people-hours than therapy, befriending and recovery programmes. To be or to medicate—that is the question.

Séamus's granny had the answer. Séamus asked his granny to mind and give him his methadone, which she diligently did each day. After about three months she went to the chemist and bought a cough bottle of the same colour. Without saying a word, she continued to give Séamus his methadone, only it was doctored. Three months later he was on pure cough mixture and no methadone. After another few months, Granny now had a full press of methadone and empty cough bottles. She timed her disclosure and said to Séamus, 'You don't need that stuff any more.' He almost had withdrawals on the spot. Then she told him what she had been doing and showed him the bottles. He is totally drug-free and methadone-free ever since. Granny, time and wisdom continue to rock the cradle, thank God.

Phil shuffled along the corridors, never lifting her slippered feet, took her medication and regressed again into a human, thumb-sucking rocking-chair. The nursing staff were kind, tired and grossly overworked. Extra medication was the only way to maintain a very understaffed ward. Phil was introduced to a befriender who called to see her every week. The visits became the centrepiece of her life. A case conference was called at the request of the befriender, which included an audit of all Phil's medication. A gradual reduction was agreed, so that Phil could be more alert on the days of her visit. Within weeks she was helping in the kitchen, lifting her once-leaden feet and sitting normally. Over a period of two years she moved from total hospitalisation to sheltered accommodation and eventually to self-contained independent living. The befriender is the cornerstone of her equilibrium and her new life.

The time of such trained volunteers has given a new lease of life to many Phils in our country. 'Can you spend one hour with me?' is as real today as it was two thousand years ago. The late Archbishop Ryan invited everyone who could to give of their time to befriend one person as their response to the Gospel challenge of Matthew 25:31–46. Those who have taken up the challenge, or similar ones, have enriched the lives of others as well as their own and have come to realise that 'it is in giving that we receive' (St Ignatius).

Wasting time with God was what some of the spiritual writers called prayer or talking to God. Real praying propels people into living their prayers through the way they treat people, especially those most in need. Phil's befriender and Séamus's granny lived their prayer through 'wasting time with people.'

A web site worth visiting is www.volunteeringireland.com.

Bishop Eamonn Walsh is an auxiliary to the Archbishop of Dublin. He is also a barrister. A native of Co. Kildare, he has extensive pastoral experience as a former chaplain to several schools and prisons. When Arbour Hill Prison, Dublin, was opened in 1975 he was appointed its first chaplain. He was also chaplain to the women's prison at Mountjoy from 1972 to 1985. He was ordained bishop in 1990 and since then has responsibility for Tallaght, Co. Dublin, together with the south-west rural and city regions. He is a member of the Communications Commission and the Bishops' Initiative on Drugs. In 2002 he was appointed apostolic administrator of the Diocese of Ferns, in conjunction with his other responsibilities; he completed this task in April 2006 and has resumed his full-time duties as auxiliary bishop in Dublin.

Quality time

Bishop Willie Walsh

I was privileged recently to spend some holiday time with an extended family that included a young couple and their 3½-year-old daughter. I believe it was the first time I really took notice of the amount of time that parents give to their children. The stories of Cinderella, of Snow White and other 'on the spot' compositions were told and retold, with the accuracy of the retelling often challenged. The thousand 'whys' were patiently answered, and I noticed how the parents never resorted to 'That's the why'!

It was clear to me that parents don't measure time given to their children. They know instinctively that such time is never time wasted. How appropriate that nowadays such time is called 'quality time'!

We never outgrow the basic human need to be given time by others. Each one of us needs to have the attention of others, to be listened to and to have our 'whys' answered, or at least acknowledged and respected. We need to relate to others and to be related to by others: 'no man is an island.' We cannot establish or sustain any relationship of quality without giving time to it. If nobody is prepared to spend time with me I cannot have any appreciation of my own worth and my own specialness.

It almost goes without saying that we live in a world where we seem to be constantly short of time. In a world that places such emphasis on efficiency, making the most of one's time is a must. We are busy at work and we are also busy making time for our leisure activities. We have so many things to get done that we have little time to spare, little time to simply 'be with' people. Parents too are finding it increasingly difficult to spend as much time with their children as they would like.

On a personal level, I find myself asking the question 'Have I any time for myself?' I don't mean this in a self-pitying way, but I do realise that I can become a victim of my own need to be busy. I can easily become a superficial responder to every perceived need of others. I need time off to reflect on the deeper things of life and to respond to my own whys and wherefores.

The Jesuit theologian Michael Paul Gallagher in a recent book entitled *Dive Deeper* devotes a chapter to 'Solitude and silence'. He speaks of our fear of depth, a fear of being-with-myself. He asks what is the tone of being-with-myself: 'Is it a shallow, almost embarrassed encounter? Or can it be a zone of presence and listening, where another kind of wisdom is learned?'

Many of us are afraid to or perhaps lack that capacity to listen to ourselves. Being busy is less threatening. Yet there is a part of all our lives where only we can enter. It is a space where I recognise that nobody else can live my life. That capacity to be-with-myself is an important antidote to the loneliness that many feel amidst the 'busy-ness' of today's world.

How about the attitude 'Talking to him or her is a waste of time?' Don't we all act that way at times, even if we don't use those exact words? It is often easier to give the couple of euros' hand-out to someone in need than to spend a little time talking to them. This may ease our discomfort when confronted with their pain, but it does little to lift them up. A few words of simple greeting or inquiry about their wellbeing might serve far better than a few euros handed over in silence. 'Ah, yes, but you see, all that takes time, and in a busy day . . .' etc.

Christ reminded us by word and example of the need to avoid that 'too-busy syndrome'. He was always escaping to quiet places to reflect and pushing out the boat to speak to people. And of course there was the time he visited the home of Martha and Mary: 'Martha, Martha, you are anxious and bothered about many things but Mary has chosen the better part and it will not be taken from her' (Luke 10:41–42). Mary had chosen to spend time with Jesus, and for her that was a life-giving experience.

We too must learn to choose the 'better part'. Spending time with others and myself is never a waste of time. It is quality time.

Bishop Willie Walsh, Bishop of Killaloe, is a native of Roscrea, Co. Tipperary. He studied for the priesthood at St Patrick's College, Maynooth, and the Irish College, Rome, and was ordained in Rome in 1959. He has been pastorally involved with Accord (formerly the Catholic Marriage Advisory Council) since its foundation in the Killaloe diocese and has worked with marriage tribunals at the diocesan, regional and national levels. He has pursued a life-long interest in sport and has been involved in coaching hurling teams at the college, club and county levels.

Wasting time

Padraig Yeates

Finding the time to write an article on 'Wasting time with people' was not easy. I spent most of my working life being paid by various newspapers to listen to people, and very often that was not easy either. Even if someone had something interesting to say there were deadlines looming, other people to listen to after them, more copy to write, more deadlines to meet.

It was not always like that. Twenty-five years ago the *Irish Times*, for instance, was quite a civilised place to work. You were not expected to arrive much before 3 p.m. and could often leave before 9 p.m. if you had a satisfactory number of stories written. In some ways it was a better newspaper than now, because the leisurely pace of work actually allowed you to listen to people and not just extract the required minimum of information from them required to write a story. You even had a chance to meet them in person, rather than commune by e-mail or telephone.

I first met Alice Leahy of TRUST in this way, in Conway's pub, maybe thirty years ago, to talk about the problems she was confronting daily amongst the homeless on Dublin's streets. At the time I worked for the *Irish People*, where the pace was somewhat more frenetic than the *Irish Times* but still allowed me space to go down to Conway's and have a civilised conversation with her on an important social problem—one that, regrettably, has not gone away.

Probably the most useful thing I ever did in journalism arose out of an opportunity that Conor O'Clery (the best news editor I ever worked for in the *Irish Times*) gave me to spend a whole month looking into the drugs scene in Dublin in 1984. It was a revelation for me, and the readers.

Today the avalanche of information, much of it pre-packed by professionals, frequently includes interviews with subjects you need never meet, be they business moguls, exploited child labourers in the Third World, or the great mass of celebrities who now seem to outnumber ordinary people. Thanks to the wonders of modern technology, you simply download, cut and paste. You may even get away with not having to read the stuff yourself before passing it on to the unfortunate reader.

The art of listening is no longer needed and rarely practised, except by professionals such as psychiatrists and counsellors. Many of the people who encounter the listening professionals have already reached an irreversible point in their lives, where a marriage has ended, an addiction triumphed or a crime been committed. Lack of communication is usually the source of most of these crises. It may seem to come from within but the critical juncture usually lies in a childhood where there were no listeners.

I have no idea how you tackle the communications deficit whose consequences now run riot through society. The only quick fix may be programmes such as Joe Duffy's wonderful 'Liveline', which, with its many faults, can still illuminate important issues for people, at both a collective and an individual level, in a way rarely achieved elsewhere.

One of the paradoxes of modern life is that with so much information to process each day we have no time to reflect on the content. Information overload has the same effect in an A&E department, the customer service section of a large company or a hostel for the homeless as it has in a newsroom. It renders it harder and harder to make sensible, people-centred decisions.

In the Middle Ages, which ended around the advent of the mobile phone and e-mail, there were institutionalised places (churches usually) and times (the Angelus, confession, retreats) that were incorporated in daily life precisely to allow for reflection—and admittedly indoctrination as well. Today churches are an endangered architectural species, and the only well-attended religious ceremonies are rites of passage, such as first communions and weddings. Celebration is the order of the day, rather than reflection, and it takes a rare priest, best man or father of the bride to make a speech worth listening to.

That is of, course, part of the problem. If we have a surfeit of information we have a deficit in quality. The media industry is, understandably, the worst offender. It is a communications tool designed to deliver agendas. Ideas, feelings and information are certainly involved, but they are part of the tool kit, subordinated to the delivery of an often very superficial message.

From my experience you need to talk to people informally and have a genuine interest in what they are doing before they open up. I spent much of my working life covering 'big', formal events, where journalists do little more than report the obvious and the superficial.

By far the best stories come from unlikely encounters: meeting a young drug-pusher and his girl-friend cowering in a flat off School Street while a crowd of Concerned Parents howled for their eviction outside, or meeting a former bomber, released after a long prison term in England, to find his parents dead and without a friend in the world because he had renounced the only organisation that might have helped him, the Provos. What good my listening to their stories did them I do not know—maybe none. Sometimes all you can do is bear witness. You don't have to be a journalist to do that, but you do have to be someone who is not rushing to meet yet another deadline.

Padraig Yeates is a former editor of the *Irish People* and senior correspondent with the *Irish Times,* now working as a media consultant and writer. His recent books include *Lockout: Dublin, 1913* (2000) and *Saving the Future,* with Tim Hastings and Brian Sheehan (2007).